Allen, John
1957-

Hitler's fina
solution.

UNDERSTANDING THE HOLOCAUST

Hitler's Final Solution

John Allen

ReferencePoint Press®

San Diego, CA

About the Author
John Allen is a writer living in Oklahoma City.

© 2016 ReferencePoint Press, Inc.
Printed in the United States

For more information, contact:
ReferencePoint Press, Inc.
PO Box 27779
San Diego, CA 92198
www. ReferencePointPress.com

LIBRARY OF CONGRESS CATALOGING-IN-PUBLICATION DATA

Allen, John, 1957- author.
  Hitler's final solution / by John Allen.
     pages cm. -- (Understanding the Holocaust series)
  Includes bibliographical references and index.
  ISBN-13: 978-1-60152-840-7 (hardback)
  ISBN-10: 1-60152-840-X (hardback)
  1. Jews--Persecutions--Germany--History--20th century--Juvenile literature. 2. Holocaust, Jewish (1939-1945)--Juvenile literature. I. Title.
  DS134.255.A3597 2016
  940.53'18--dc23

                                                              2014043334

CONTENTS

IMPORTANT EVENTS OF THE HOLOCAUST

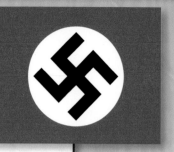

1937
Buchenwald concentration camp is established in east-central Germany.

1941
Germany invades the Soviet Union; the Germans massacre about one hundred thousand Jews, Roma (Gypsies), Communists, and others at Babi Yar in Ukraine; the United States declares war on Japan and Germany after Japan attacks Pearl Harbor.

1920
The Nazi Party publishes its 25-point program declaring its intention to segregate Jews from so-called Aryan society and to eliminate the political, legal, and civil rights of Germany's Jewish population.

1925
Adolf Hitler's autobiographical manifesto *Mein Kampf* is published; in it he outlines his political ideology and future plans for Germany and calls for the violent elimination of the world's Jews.

1940
The Warsaw ghetto—a 1.3 square mile (3.4 sq km) area sealed off from the rest of the city by high walls, barbed wire, and armed guards—is established in Poland.

1920 / 1934   1936   1938   1940

1918
The Treaty of Versailles, marking the formal end of World War I and a humiliating defeat for Germany, is signed.

1935
The Nuremberg Laws, excluding German Jews from citizenship and depriving them of the right to vote and hold public office, are enacted.

1939
Germany invades Poland, igniting World War II in Europe; in Warsaw, Jews are forced to wear white armbands with a blue Star of David.

1933
Hitler is appointed Germany's chancellor; the Gestapo is formed; Dachau concentration camp is established.

1938
Violent anti-Jewish attacks known as *Kristallnacht* (Night of Broken Glass) take place throughout greater Germany; the first *Kindertransport* (children's transport) arrives in Great Britain with thousands of Jewish children seeking refuge from Nazi persecution.

4

1942

The Nazi plan to annihilate Europe's Jews (the Final Solution) is outlined at the Wannsee Conference in Berlin; deportations of about 1.5 million Jews to killing centers in Poland begin.

1944

Allied forces carry out the D-Day invasion at Normandy in France; diplomats in Budapest offer protection to Jews.

1948

The State of Israel is established as a homeland for the world's Jews.

1946

The International Military Tribunal imposes death and prison sentences during the Nuremberg Trials.

1949

Argentina grants asylum to Josef Mengele, the notorious SS doctor who performed medical experiments on prisoners in Auschwitz.

1942   1944   1946   1948 / 1970

1943

Despite armed Jewish resistance, the Nazis move to liquidate ghettos in Poland and the Soviet Union; Denmark actively resists Nazi attempts to deport its Jewish citizens.

1960

In Argentina, Israeli intelligence agents abduct Adolf Eichmann, one of the masterminds of the Holocaust; he is brought to Israel to stand trial for crimes against the Jewish people.

1945

Allied forces liberate Auschwitz, Buchenwald, and Dachau concentration camps; Hitler commits suicide; World War II ends with the surrender of Germany and Japan; the Nuremberg Trials begin with war crimes indictments against leading Nazis.

1981

More than ten thousand survivors attend the first World Gathering of Jewish Holocaust Survivors in Israel; a similar gathering two years later in Washington, DC, attracts twenty thousand people.

1947

The UN General Assembly adopts a resolution partitioning Palestine into Jewish and Arab states; Holocaust survivor Simon Wiesenthal opens a center in Austria to search for Nazis who have evaded justice.

A Speech on an Age-Old Hatred

At a Berlin rally on September 14, 2014, German chancellor Angela Merkel delivered a powerful speech on an age-old problem. To a crowd numbering in the thousands Merkel pledged that her government would do its utmost to oppose anti-Semitism and prevent violence against Jews. "Anyone who hits someone wearing a skullcap is hitting us all," she said. "Anyone who damages a Jewish gravestone is disgracing our culture. Anyone who attacks a synagogue is attacking the foundations of our free society. . . . It hurts me when I hear that young Jewish parents are asking if it's safe to raise their children here or elderly ask if it was right to stay here."[1] Merkel's speech came after a summer filled with anti-Semitic incidents in Germany. Street protesters opposed to Israel's war in Gaza had shouted "Jews to the gas!"[2]—referring to gas chambers in the Nazi death camps during World War II. Molotov cocktails had set synagogues ablaze, and scrawled swastikas had appeared on Jewish gravestones. Similar outrages occurred elsewhere in Europe at the same time, yet the German incidents seemed especially ominous. They hearkened back to the virulent anti-Semitism of the Nazi regime and to Hitler's so-called Final Solution, the attempt to systematically murder all the Jews of Europe.

A Murderous Campaign in Stages

Mass murder of Jews did not begin at once when Hitler and the Nazis assumed power in 1933. In fact the Nazi campaign against Jews unfolded in rough stages. At first there were laws to exclude Jews from the social and economic life of the nation. Next came a period of persecution in which Jews were robbed of their wealth and property, Jewish businesses were attacked, and synagogues were defaced and torched. After 1938, when German troops began their conquest of Europe, huge numbers of Jews fell under Nazi control. Hitler and his henchmen instituted a policy of deporting captured Jews to ghettos and concentration camps in eastern Europe, mostly in Poland. Mobile death squads slaughtered whole villages of Jews, dumping the victims in mass graves. Finally, during the invasion of the Soviet Union, the Nazis devised the Final Solution: a plan to turn concentration camps into efficient killing factories, gassing helpless Jews by the thousands. That this plan, this grandiose scheme to exterminate Europe's Jews, not only was put into effect but nearly succeeded remains one of the most chilling facts of the modern age.

The scale of the Final Solution was massive. Between 1938 and 1945 the Nazis murdered more than six million Jews. It is easy to blame this crime on the twisted mind of one man, Adolf Hitler. A frustrated artist and political gadfly, Hitler was steeped in the ideas of his time, including the anti-Semitism that was common among certain of his fellow Austrians. Hitler's burning ambition to avenge Germany's humiliating defeat in the Great War, which he blamed largely on the Jews, and unite the so-called Aryan race into a new Germany was stoked by political pamphlets and Germanic myths gleaned from operas. Hitler was a powerful speaker who could mesmerize crowds with his hateful rhetoric. Nevertheless, the German people themselves—from Nazi officials to soldiers who claimed to be merely following orders to civilians who shrugged

> "I only took part in the murder of three million people out of consideration for my family."[3]
>
> —Head of the political department, Auschwitz death camp.

at the daily outrages against Jews—must bear a large measure of responsibility. Most never questioned their assigned tasks. And many agreed with the Nazis' program to rid the world of Jews, viewing it as a necessary step to an improved future. As the head of the political department at the Auschwitz death camp wrote, "I only took part in the murder of three million people out of consideration for my family."[3] It is obvious that the Final Solution could not have happened had anti-Semitism not been so firmly rooted in German society and in Europe as a whole.

Nazi troops with bicycles parade before Adolf Hitler at a 1933 rally. A powerful speaker, Hitler mesmerized crowds with his hateful rhetoric wherever he went.

Jews' Major Role in German Society

Before the Nazis rose to power Jews in Germany and Austria were better assimilated than those in other European countries. Jewish individuals played a major role in literature and the arts, banking and finance, science and industry. Many considered themselves as thoroughly German as any of their neighbors. In a 1912 essay, writer Moritz Goldstein insisted, "The German spring is our spring as the German winter is for us winter. . . . Are not the German forests alive for us? . . . Do we not understand the murmur of its streams and the song of its birds?"[4] Such feelings explain why many German and Austrian Jews were at first slow to realize the extent of the danger they faced from Hitler's murderous regime.

As Allied troops liberated the death camps at the end of World War II they photographed the awful evidence of genocide. Since 1945 the world has seen other attempts at genocide, but there have also been efforts to educate people about the Nazi horrors and prevent another Final Solution. In Merkel's speech she refers to the almost miraculous fact that more than one hundred thousand Jews are now living in Germany. In 1948 Israel declared its independence as a Jewish state and a haven for Jews. In 1993 the United States Holocaust Memorial Museum was dedicated in Washington, DC, as a tribute to the Holocaust's victims and a remembrance of how it unfolded. In 2006 the United Nations created the Advisory Committee on Genocide Prevention, and the UN continues to monitor human rights violations around the world. To ensure that an episode like the Final Solution never happens again, it is necessary to be vigilant and remember.

CHAPTER ONE

Hatred and Exclusion

In 1933 Adolf Hitler and the Nazi Party rose to power in Germany pushing an ideology based on anti-Semitism, or hatred of Jews. This deeply held prejudice was hardly novel. It dated back hundreds of years to the Middle Ages and even earlier. Jews were blamed for Christ's death and reviled as treacherous conspirators. They were periodically subjected to violent mob attacks, called pogroms, in European cities and towns. Usually these attacks sought to punish Jews for somehow causing an outbreak of plague or some other disaster. Intimidated by leaders of church and state and fearing violence from Christian mobs, Jews were forced to separate themselves, band together in tight communities, and keep a low profile. In many countries Jews could not perform certain jobs or hold certain kinds of property. Often they were confined to specific areas, called ghettos. Even Jews who converted to Christianity were frequently ostracized and looked on with suspicion. Governments and church officials used sources such as Protestant reformer Martin Luther's 1542 screed against Jews and the latter-day forgery *The Protocols of the Elders of Zion* to justify their anti-Semitism. In the late 1800s politicians and writers perpetuated the slanders against Jews. Thus Hitler and the Nazis were merely building on a form of hatred familiar to all Germans and shared by many.

The Rise of Hitler and National Socialism

Hitler's vicious anti-Semitism blossomed after World War I. He blamed Jewish financiers for forcing Germany to accept the humiliating terms of the Treaty of Versailles. He also hated communism, which he believed was an inferior form of socialism and a tool of a worldwide Jewish conspiracy. Overall he saw Jews as the reason Germany had lost the war and as a pernicious influence bringing civilized nations to ruin.

In reality many German Jews had fought bravely in the war, and Jews represented only a tiny percentage of Europe's population.

In 1919, one year after the war's end, Hitler joined a political group that became the National Socialist German Workers' Party, or Nazi Party. Hitler, who had been a failure as a painter and an aimless knock-about since the war, found his one talent. He quickly became the group's most popular speaker, able to mesmerize an audience with his impassioned warnings about Jews and traitorous politicians. He blamed Jews for the weak postwar economy, massive unemployment, and runaway inflation. His speeches were comforting to Germans seeking a scapegoat for their troubles. From the beginning Hitler's long-term goals were not in doubt. "Anti-Semitism based purely on emotion will find its ultimate expression in pogroms," he said in 1919. "But anti-Semitism based on reason must lead to the organized, legal campaign and removal of Jewish privileges. Its ultimate, unshakeable goal must be the elimination of the Jews."5

> "Anti-Semitism based on reason must lead to the organized, legal campaign and removal of Jewish privileges. Its ultimate, unshakeable goal must be the elimination of the Jews."5
>
> —Adolf Hitler, 1919.

In November 1923 Hitler was arrested for his role in the Beer Hall Putsch, a failed attempt to seize control of the German government. While in prison, he wrote the first part of *Mein Kampf*, which means "my struggle." The book combines memoir and propaganda, mixing self-serving lies about Hitler's life story with diatribes about parasitic Jews and the need for racial purity in Germany. Hitler raises the idea of *lebensraum*, or space for expansion of the united German people. He also presents his belief in social Darwinism, a central tenet of Nazi ideology. He insists that evolution can be engineered to produce superior individuals and eliminate weaker elements that are polluting the gene pool. In the book's second part, published in 1927, Hitler reviews the recent history of the Nazi movement and specifies how he will accomplish his goals. He even candidly admits how he will dupe the public with his program:

> All propaganda must be popular and its intellectual level must be adjusted to the most limited intelligence among those it is addressed to. Consequently, the greater the mass it is intended

to reach, the lower its purely intellectual level will have to be. ... The art of propaganda lies in understanding the emotional ideas of the great masses and finding, through a psychologically correct form, the way to the attention and thence to the heart of the broad masses.[6]

By January 1933, when Hitler became chancellor, he was fully prepared to put his plans into action. The Nazi Party he led drew much of its support from the lower middle class and peasantry, who

Hitler wrote Mein Kampf *while in prison for his role in a failed coup attempt. Part memoir and part propaganda, the book contains self-serving lies and diatribes about Jews and the need for racial purity in Germany.*

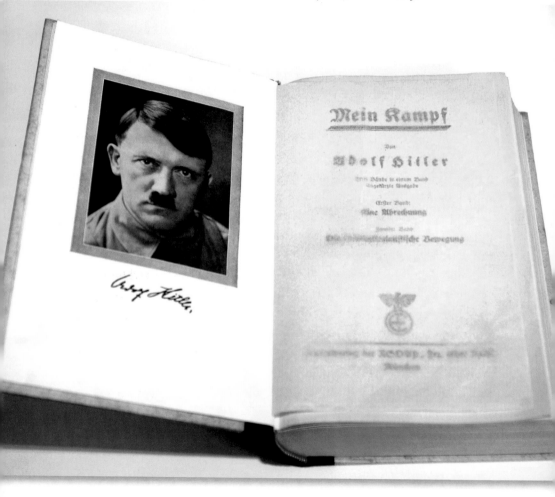

were strongly nationalistic and more susceptible to arguments that Jews were wrecking the country. Hitler rapidly wiped out other political parties and consolidated his position as dictator. He wasted no time in using his new power to harass the nation's Jews.

Boycott of Businesses Owned by Jews

Soon after seizing power the Nazis swore in forty thousand storm troopers and SS men as auxiliary police. Roaming the streets of major cities, they began to settle scores with Jews and political foes. They assaulted victims in the back rooms of restaurants, in factories and breweries, and on board ships. Reports on these attacks and other acts of intimidation appeared in the foreign press. Hitler and Joseph Goebbels, his minister of propaganda, claimed these anti-German stories were being spread by an international conspiracy of Jews. In response, they decided to organize a nationwide boycott of businesses owned by Jews. The boycott took place on April 1, 1933. It did not have the force of law, but the Nazis went to great lengths to get people to follow their lead. Uniformed thugs, truncheons in hand, loitered menacingly outside Jewish-owned stores and the offices of Jewish doctors and lawyers. Stars of David and anti-Semitic slogans were painted on shop windows. Passersby were discouraged from entering. Those who defied the boycott were photographed and tabbed as troublemakers. In Leipzig, Jewish businesspeople were forced to march down the center of a commercial street holding large signs that read, "Don't buy from Jews; Shop in German businesses!"[7]

"All propaganda must be popular and its intellectual level must be adjusted to the most limited intelligence among those it is addressed to. Consequently, the greater the mass it is intended to reach, the lower its purely intellectual level will have to be."[6]

—Adolf Hitler, in *Mein Kampf*.

Goebbels claimed that support for the boycott was widespread. Yet many Germans, still unfamiliar with Nazi tactics, reacted with shock. They never thought they would be prevented from shopping at their favorite stores. Scuffles broke out when some defiantly refused to follow the ban. As for Jewish shop owners, they suddenly felt as if they were stranded in a foreign land. In one town a bitter Jewish war veteran stood outside his family's department store dressed in his military uniform and medals. He passed out leaflets that reminded people about the twelve thousand Jewish soldiers who had lost their lives fighting for Germany in the Great War. The Nazi-led boycott lasted only a day, but it was a grim portent of what was to come.

Removal of Jews from Civil Service and Other Jobs

A week after the boycott the Nazis announced a new law concerning the civil service, or the German bureaucracy. The law's supposed purpose was to get rid of government workers appointed by the prior regime. In reality it forced Jews, defined as anyone with a Jewish grandparent, to retire from the civil service at once. Another law disbarred more than fourteen hundred Jewish lawyers and almost four hundred judges and prosecutors. More than twenty-five hundred government-employed Jewish doctors in schools, hospitals, and welfare agencies lost their jobs within the year. Aryan women were warned to avoid Jewish physicians. Jewish pathologists were not allowed to examine non-Jewish corpses. Alarmed by the rising tide of anti-Semitism, two hundred of Germany's Jewish academics, one-fourth the estimated total, left the country. Many of these men and women were known worldwide, and twenty of them, including Albert Einstein, had won the Nobel Prize. Similar flights occurred in the theater, cinema, literature, painting, and journalism. Few non-Jews protested this exodus, perhaps because they coveted the vacant positions or saw a chance for advancement with their competitors out of the way. As the physicist Max Planck observed, "If today thirty professors get up and protest against the government's actions, by tomorrow there will be 150 individuals declaring their solidarity with Hitler, simply because they're after the jobs."[8]

By May 1935 the Nazis had passed laws prohibiting Jews from owning farmland, joining labor unions, and obtaining national health insurance. The creation of the Reich Chamber of Culture enabled Nazi promoters to exclude Jews from the arts and cultural events. Jews could no longer apply for a law license or serve in the military. Public book burnings, in which pro-Nazi crowds cheered as banned volumes were tossed onto huge bonfires, focused on works by Jewish authors. Beatings of Jews were rampant, and many Jews committed suicide in despair.

Hitler and Eugenics

Adolf Hitler plainly stated his goal of eliminating Jews in order to purify Germany's racial stock. Nazi policy promoted higher birth rates for so-called Aryans, whom the Nazis considered racially pure Germans. At the same time, mixed marriages with people labeled as inferior were discouraged or even outlawed. Such ideas did not originate with Hitler and the Nazis. They were rooted in the pseudoscience of eugenics, which had many believers in the early twentieth century. The word *eugenics* comes from Greek roots meaning "good origin." Eugenics sought to improve the genetic quality of the human race by eliminating those considered unfit or somehow inferior. Followers of eugenics wanted to sterilize people they thought inferior to prevent them from breeding and polluting the gene pool. Some went further, advocating the deaths of unwanted individuals.

Eugenics of course was racist from the beginning. It was often raised as an argument against immigrants in Western nations. Margaret Sanger, the American founder of the birth control movement, believed in eugenics and thought birth control would result in fewer children from the unfit. Eugenics also won support from many intellectuals. In 1933 the Irish playwright George Bernard Shaw wrote, "Extermination must be put on a scientific basis if it is ever to be carried out humanely. . . . If we desire a certain type of civilization and culture we must exterminate the sort of people who do not fit into it." Such beliefs were just steps away from the Nazi death camps.

Quoted in Daniel Hannan, "Leftists Become Incandescent When Reminded of the Socialist Roots of Nazism," *Telegraph*, February 25, 2014. http://blogs.telegraph.co.uk.

To win favor with the Nazis, non-Jews took measures of their own. College administrators fired professors with Jewish wives or those whose parents had converted from Judaism. Schoolteachers harassed Jewish students and turned a blind eye to abuse by their classmates. Some business owners fired employees known to have

Young Nazis cheer and salute in 1933 in Berlin as they burn thousands of books, many written by Jewish authors. Anti-Jewish sentiments were soon bolstered by laws that, among other things, prohibited Jews from owning farmland, joining labor unions, and obtaining health insurance.

romantic relationships with Jews. When local officials began to drop Jews from welfare rolls, the national government also adopted the practice. Jews were steadily being excluded from every aspect of German life.

The Nuremberg Race Laws

To reinforce the exclusion of Jews, Hitler announced the Nuremberg Race Laws at the annual party rally in 1935. Hitler claimed the laws were necessary to stop the "defensive actions of the enraged population"[9]—a rage that he and his henchmen did everything to inflame. The laws effectively put Jews at the mercy of the state. As the historian Nathan Stoltzfus writes:

These laws, a watershed in the evolution of Nazi racial policy, a major step on the way to the Holocaust, were to deprive Jews of their citizenship and basic rights. For the announcement of such a radical departure from recent German legal and social traditions, what occasion could be more accommodating than the annual party rally held in Nuremberg? By 1935 there was no better platform for portraying Hitler as the great charismatic leader, and on this occasion he aligned his popularity with anti-Semitism by giving the first major public speech on the Jewish Question since becoming reich chancellor.[10]

Bureaucrats had hastily drafted and redrafted the two new laws to please the Führer (leader). Parts of one law were initially scribbled on the back of a menu. Yet the new measures would soon wreck lives across the European continent. The Reich Citizenship Law deprived German Jews of all rights of citizenship in Hitler's empire, or *Reich*. Under the new law Jews were considered subjects with obligations to the state but no rights. A later addition spelled out that Jews were not allowed to vote or hold public office. The Law for the Protection of German Blood and German Honor prohibited Jews from marrying or having sexual relations with persons of German or related blood. This law also defined a Jew not by the individual's religious beliefs but by family relationships. Anyone who had three or four Jewish grandparents was automatically labeled a Jew, regardless of whether the person observed Jewish religious customs or belonged to the Jewish religious community. Conversion to Christianity had no effect. Even secular Jews were immediately subject to Nazi persecution. The law also forbade Jews to employ Aryan housekeepers or fly the national flag. For the world press, Hitler claimed the Race Laws would help Germans maintain tolerable relations with the Jewish people. In reality Jews were to be considered a foreign element in the people's midst.

> "[The Nuremberg Race Laws], a watershed in the evolution of Nazi racial policy, a major step on the way to the Holocaust, were to deprive Jews of their citizenship and basic rights."[10]
>
> —Historian Nathan Stoltzfus.

Due to past intermarriages, the Nuremberg Race Laws caused considerable confusion in German society. Hitler had opted for a version of the laws that left out the last line: "This law applies only to full-blooded Jews."[11] Many Germans were suddenly worried about being classified as Jews. The Nazi Party itself considered anyone with Jewish blood to be of a lower status. Yet government officials feared the repercussions if people who considered themselves loyal Germans were suddenly ostracized for having Jewish ancestry. Such persons included highly decorated veterans of the Great War and distinguished backers of the Nazi regime. Strict enforcement could have cost the military as many as forty-five thousand current soldiers. Sanctioning citizens married to Jews was also a potential powder keg because of the German respect for marriage. Faced with these dilemmas, the Nazis issued a series of addenda to the Race Laws, defining the levels of Jewishness. Having three or more Jewish grandparents classified a person as a full Jew. With two Jewish grandparents a person was considered a first-degree *Mischling* (crossbreed), or half Jew. One Jewish grandparent made one a *Mischling* of the second degree, or quarter Jew. About 350,000 Germans were classified as *Mischlinge* (plural of *Mischling*). Of this total about 50,000 were Christian converts, 220,000 half Jews, and 80,000 quarter Jews. Each status carried its own drawbacks both socially and in the workplace. Officials tried to educate the public about this absurd system with complicated charts. Yet Nazi bureaucrats themselves could not agree on how strictly to enforce the laws. The Nuremberg Laws of the supposedly ultra-efficient Nazis became a bureaucratic nightmare of loopholes, second thoughts, and red tape.

Effects of the Race Laws

For all their outrageousness, the Nuremberg Race Laws actually drew the support of many Jews. What had been open season on acts of violence or mischief against them now became a more orderly situation. Jews were relieved to at least know what boundaries they had to observe in their daily lives. Peter Gaupp, who was considered a half Jew, explained:

> In 1935, the laws came out, the Nuremberg Laws. That was the first time you knew where you stood legally. . . . Before it

Julius Streicher and *Der Stürmer*

Anti-Jewish propaganda in Germany sank to new depths in the pages of *Der Stürmer* ("The Attacker"). This newspaper was the work of Julius Streicher, one of Hitler's earliest supporters. Named a regional party boss as reward for his loyalty, Streicher was obsessed with spreading his anti-Semitic views. He began publishing his newspaper in 1923, and four years later it had a weekly circulation of almost fifteen thousand copies. When the Nazis came to power in 1933 *Der Stürmer* intensified its anti-Jewish bile. Streicher knew he could count on Nazi solidarity for protection—he even affected a small, Hitlerian mustache himself.

Der Stürmer's editorial policy is summed up in its slogan: "The Jews Are Our Misfortune." The crudity of its message was matched by its content. Like today's supermarket tabloids, each issue focused on stories about sex, crime, and lurid scandal. Stories were written in a simplistic style, with short sentences and common words, and accused Jews of everything from tax evasion to the murder of children. *Der Stürmer* was known for its cartoons, which depicted Jews with exaggerated features or as snakes, spiders, and vermin. Often Jews were shown attacking young blonde Aryan women, whose carefully drawn nude bodies were one of the paper's main attractions. By 1938 the paper had achieved a circulation approaching a half million. Copies appeared each week in special display cases at bus stops and on street corners, surrounded by gawking crowds. *Der Stürmer*'s anti-Semitic content was so crude that even many upper-level Nazis disapproved.

Quoted in Jennifer Rosenberg, "Der Stuermer," About Education. http://history1900s .about.com.

was all guesswork. You could meet a Nazi in some office and he could exterminate you or you could meet a Nazi that was very human and he could help you. . . . Before 1935, before the laws came out of Nuremberg, you swam your way through. . . . You know, there was no regulations.[12]

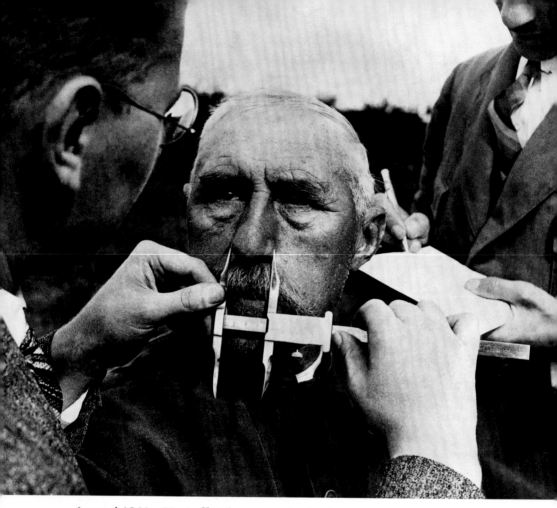

Around 1941 a Nazi official uses a pair of calipers to measure the nose of an ethnic German. The Nazis developed various schemes and charts for determining who was a Jew and who was an Aryan.

Reactions to the laws varied among non-Jews. The Catholic Church expressed disapproval but hoped the laws would curb the Nazis' more violent excesses. Protestant sermons protesting the laws were delivered—and then confiscated—in several German towns. Liberal intellectuals were appalled at the crudity of the measures. Yet many Germans, by no means hardened anti-Semites themselves, regarded the Nuremberg Laws with indifference. They seemed satisfied that the laws would have little impact on their own lives. Outside Germany the reaction was also muted. Many countries chose to ignore the whole business, taking the line that a nation should be free to decide its own questions of citizenship.

More than seventy-five thousand Jews had fled Germany by the time of the Nuremberg Race Laws. Those who stayed either thought the Nazi regime would soon collapse or figured they could maintain a low profile and get by somehow. Passage of the laws marked the end of the first phase of Nazism, a revolutionary period filled with random violence. Leading up to the Berlin Olympic Games of 1936—in which German Jews were banned from participating—Hitler and the Nazis eased some of their anti-Jewish attacks and sought to present the world a sanitized view of the regime. For a time Jews could go about their daily lives in relative security. However, this lull would prove distressingly brief.

CHAPTER TWO

Persecution

On November 8, 1937, the German Museum in Munich hosted the opening of a new exhibition titled "The Eternal Jew." Paired with a display of mostly Jewish-made "degenerate art"—the Nazis' term to describe modern art they disliked—the exhibition presented anti-Semitic images of Jews as moneychangers and swindlers. The advertising poster depicted a bearded Jew in a Middle Eastern–style caftan, holding gold coins in one hand, a whip in the other, and a map of Europe under his arm, the map imprinted with the Communist symbol of the hammer and sickle. Jews were portrayed as having always been justifiably outcast through the centuries. Now they were conspirators who sought to wreck German society with crooked finance or with communism. Photographs and drawings in the exhibit mocked the supposed ugliness of Jewish features. More than five thousand visitors a day viewed this exhibit of Nazi propaganda. As the show moved from city to city, police reports described a rise in anti-Semitic violence.

Anschluss and Renewed Oppression of Jews

"The Eternal Jew" exhibition was a prelude to a renewal of Nazi attacks on Jews. On March 12, 1938, German troops entered Austria. Hitler immediately announced the *Anschluss*, or union, of Germany and Austria. While some Germans worried that the move, which violated the postwar Treaty of Versailles, might provoke European countries to war, large majorities on both sides of the Austrian border welcomed it. Austrian crowds greeted the German troops with ringing church bells, red flags with swastikas, and Nazi salutes. The *Anschluss* brought two hundred thousand Austrian Jews under Nazi control. Most of these people lived in Vienna, one of Europe's most cultured cities, where they represented 15 percent of the population. Like their German counterparts in Berlin and Munich five years before, Austria's Jews considered themselves ordinary citizens, as patriotic as their non-Jewish neighbors. The government of Kurt von Schuschnigg had not been particularly well disposed toward Jews, but daily life had been tolerable. With the arrival of the Nazis, however, Jews were shocked at how quickly much of the populace turned on them. "What happened in Germany over five years happened in Vienna in five days," recalls one Viennese Jew. "We had no idea that we would face such violence."[13]

Soon after the *Anschluss* pro-Nazi students attacked Jewish professors and students at Viennese universities. In the streets of Vienna Jews were hauled outside at random and forced onto their hands and knees to scrub anti-Nazi slo-

> "What happened in Germany over five years happened in Vienna in five days. We had no idea that we would face such violence."[13]
>
> — Jew living in Vienna, Austria, during the 1938 *Anschluss*.

gans off the sidewalks. To the taunts of the crowd, some were handed toothbrushes to make the task more humiliating. Boys in the uniforms of Hitler Youth chased Jews through the streets and forced them to leap into the Danube canal. As the Austrian writer Stefan Zweig recalled:

> Now there was no longer mere robbery and theft, but every private lust for revenge was given free rein. University professors were obliged to scrub the streets with their naked hands, pious white-bearded Jews were dragged into the synagogue by hooting youths and forced to do knee exercises and to shout "Heil Hitler" in chorus. Innocent people in the streets were trapped like rabbits and herded off to clean the latrines in the SA barracks. All the sickly, unclean fantasies of hate that had been conceived in the course of many nights found raging expression in broad daylight.[14]

Pro-Nazi Austrians who believed their country was entering an equal partnership with Hitler were badly mistaken. Hitler moved quickly to absorb Austria into the German nation, outlawing use of the name *Austria* and cutting ties between Vienna and the country's provincial towns. Heinrich Himmler's SS, an elite military force, was

The promotional poster for the 1937 exhibit "The Eternal Jew" used anti-Semitic imagery to attract visitors. The poster depicts a big-nosed, bearded Jew with gold coins, a whip, and a map of Europe imprinted with the Communist hammer and sickle.

assigned control of Jewish affairs in Austria, and Nazi bureaucrat Adolf Eichmann set up an Office for Jewish Emigration in Vienna. With the help of local Nazis, SS troops rounded up Hitler's Austrian opponents and critics, including Social- ists, Communists, and many prominent Jews. More than thirty thousand Jews were hauled off to jail or sent to concen- tration camps, including Dachau across the border in Bavaria. Nazi rule meant Austria's Jews immediately fell under the Nuremberg Race Laws and all the other anti-Semitic measures passed

"All the sickly, unclean fantasies of hate that had been conceived in the course of many nights found raging expression in broad daylight."[14]

—Austrian writer Stefan Zweig.

in Germany. Austria also became the testing ground for even more extreme racial policies that would soon be implemented in all Nazi- controlled territory.

Registration of Wealth and Property

New laws in so-called greater Germany, which now included Austria, required Jews to add up the value of all their assets and register it with the state. These assets included real estate, bank accounts, stocks and bonds, insurance policies, and personal belongings. The first declara- tions totaled more than $800 million. While Nazi planners contem- plated how best to plunder these assets to pay for war preparations, many Nazis found ways to line their own pockets with stolen Jew- ish wealth. Nazi official Martin Bormann believed Jewish property should be given directly to "suffering" Nazi Party members:

> The transfer of Jewish businesses to German hands gives the Party the opportunity to proceed with a healthy policy. . . . It is the Party's duty of honor to support Party comrades who, because of their membership, have suffered economic disad- vantages and to help them achieve an independent livelihood. . . . It is the Party's duty to ensure that the Jew does not receive an inappropriately high purchase price. In this way, Jewry will make reparation for part of the damage that it has done to the German people.[15]

To this point economic pressure on Jews had been mostly unofficial. They had been given the option of turning their businesses over to German hands, and many had done so in hope of avoiding further trouble. However, the new phase of economic persecution after the *Anschluss* was compulsory. Hastily written laws and policies brought about the rapid and reckless Aryanization of property owned by Jews. Businesses owned by Jews had to be registered with Nazi authorities. The Nazis prohibited non-Jews from acting as fronts for Jewish business owners. Jews were banned from trading and offering certain commercial services. All Jews over the age of fifteen had to obtain an identity card and be prepared to show it to any police officer. Jewish individuals had to add a special name to their own—Sarah for women, Israel for men—when they signed legal documents in order to identify themselves as Jews. They were also prohibited from practicing law or medicine in any capacity. Jews' passports had to be stamped with a large red *J*. Overall, the Nazis aimed to cut off Jews from the economic life of the nation and prepare them for whatever schemes of isolation or removal the regime might develop.

The Night of Broken Glass

Fresh from his success with the *Anschluss*, Hitler next moved to annex the Sudetenland, an area of Czechoslovakia near the German border. French and British representatives at the Munich Conference in September 1938 agreed to the takeover, justifying it by the number of ethnic Germans in the disputed area. It was hoped that Hitler would be appeased by this concession and war could be averted. Instead the episode emboldened the Nazis and led to a new, more aggressive phase of anti-Semitism.

In October 1938 the Nazis expelled fourteen thousand Polish Jews who were living in Germany. The move was in response to Poland's demand that its Jewish citizens living outside the country renew their passports or forfeit their right to return. Polish authorities then refused entry to Polish Jews dumped at the border, forcing them into a refugee camp. Roman Grynspan, a seventeen-year-old Polish Jew living illegally in Paris, was outraged to learn that his family, including his parents who had resided in Germany for more than twenty-five years and his two sisters, were among those stuck in a holding area near the border. Grynspan went to the German embassy and shot Ernst vom Rath, a German official there. Vom Rath's death two days later coincided with the anniversary of the Nazis' Beer Hall Putsch in 1923. Gathered in Munich for the commemoration, Hitler and his top Nazi officials decided to use the shooting as a pretext for a night of frenzied violence against Jews. In a tirade to the assembled leaders, propaganda minister Joseph Goebbels blamed the killing on a worldwide Jewish conspiracy and advised retaliation. "The Fuhrer has decided," he said, "that . . . demonstrations should not be prepared

In 1938 in Vienna, Austria, a gleeful crowd gathers to watch elderly Jews forced to scrub the street on hands and knees. To make the task even more humiliating than it already was, some were forced to use toothbrushes.

Nazi Confiscation of the Wealth of Jews

It has long been known that Hitler and the Nazis looted the wealth of Jews as a prelude to the Final Solution. However, a recent study commissioned by the German government shows that the confiscated wealth also financed a large part of the Nazi war effort. In all, Nazi officials plundered 120 billion reichsmarks—about $15 billion—through confiscation policies, tax laws, and simple theft. Hans-Peter Ullmann, a Cologne University history professor who led the three-year study, said tax offices under the Nazis actively worked to "destroy Jews financially." Jews who managed to escape Germany before the worst of the Final Solution had to pay enormous exit taxes. Nazi officials also confiscated and sold the possessions of Jews deported to the east, resulting in huge profits. As Ullmann notes, "Conservatively, their money financed at least 30 percent of the German war effort."

Members of the study commission received access to government documents that revealed how Nazi bureaucrats carried out the theft. Christine Kuller, a University of Munich professor who also worked on the investigation, says Nazi tax offices set up special levels of bureaucrats to ferret out Jewish wealth in dwellings and bank accounts. Auctions were regularly held to dispose of furniture, artwork, and other possessions seized from Jewish homes. "Post war there was a myth that the civil servants of the finance ministry were neutral," Kuller says. "The reality was that anti-Semitism among them was an everyday occurrence."

Quoted in Allan Hall, "Confiscated Jewish Wealth 'Helped Fund the German War Effort,'" *Telegraph*, November 9, 2010. www.telegraph.co.uk.

or organized by the Party, but insofar as they erupt spontaneously, they are not to be hampered."[16]

The result was a Nazi-endorsed pogrom of unprecedented scale. Regional party officials sent word to local offices, which ordered police to arrest young Jewish males but not to interfere otherwise. By the late evening of November 9 and continuing till dawn, Nazi thugs rampaged through the cities and towns of the *Reich*, torching synagogues and vandalizing Jewish homes, businesses, and cemeteries. Crowds watched the synagogues burn, and firefighters stood by to act only if nearby property of non-Jews was threatened. Gangs of storm troopers and Hitler Youth, many dressed in civilian clothes to disguise the violence as a spontaneous uprising, broke into the homes of Jews, brutally attacking them and forcing them to perform humiliating acts in the streets. Certain male Jews were targeted by Nazi zealots and knifed or battered to death in front of their families. Mobs smashed windows and looted merchandise in thousands of shops and businesses owned by Jews throughout Germany, Austria, and Sudetenland. With heaps of glass shards lying everywhere on streets and sidewalks, the night of rioting became known as *Kristallnacht* (the night of crystal), or the night of broken glass. Armin Hertz was fourteen and living with his divorced mother in Berlin at the time of the attacks. He remembers the night and its aftermath:

> "Our store was destroyed, glass was broken, the synagogues were set on fire. There was a synagogue in the same street where we lived. . . . They threw everything out of the window—the Torah scrolls, the prayer books, the benches, everything."[17]
>
> —Armin Hertz, a Berlin Jew who, at age fourteen, witnessed *Kristallnacht*.

Our store was destroyed, glass was broken, the synagogues were set on fire. There was a synagogue in the same street where we lived. . . . They threw everything out of the window—the Torah scrolls, the prayer books, the benches, everything. . . . As I was riding along the business district, I saw all the stores destroyed, windows broken, everything lying in the street. They were even going into the stores and running away with the merchandise. Finally, I got to my aunt's house and I saw a large crowd assembled in front of the store. The fire department was there; the police were there. The fire department was pouring water on the adjacent building. The synagogue in the back was on fire, but they were not putting the water on the synagogue. The police were there watching it.[17]

Passersby peer into shops that were destroyed and looted during Kristallnacht (night of broken glass), a wave of violent attacks that took place on November 9–10, 1938. The attacks—orchestrated by Hitler and other top Nazi officials—destroyed Jewish homes, shops, and synagogues.

While pretending that the pogrom was unplanned, the Nazis actually set certain limits on the rioting at the start. Foreigners, including Jews, were declared off limits, and the property of non-Jews was supposed to be protected. The orgy of violence proved beneficial to Nazi morale. One report by an elite SS commander declared, "All troops and leaders took great delight in the action. Such orders should be given more often."[18]

Reactions to *Kristallnacht*

The wave of violence resulted in grim statistics: 91 Jews murdered, 30,000 Jews arrested and sent to concentration camps, 7,500 shops and businesses owned by Jews vandalized and looted, more than 1,000 synagogues burned. Three days later Hermann Goering, a member of Hitler's inner circle, told a meeting of party leaders that Jews were to blame for the violence. The Jewish community would be forced to pay the equivalent of $400 million for the death of the German diplomat in Paris and another $100 million for property damage. Insurance payments went straight into government coffers. Goering declared that Jews were officially banned from the German economy. He also announced, "I have received a letter written on the Fuhrer's orders requesting that the Jewish question be now, once and for all, coordinated and solved one way or another."[19] Thus *Kristallnacht* was a crucial step toward the Final Solution.

The economic ban left many Jews destitute and even more vulnerable to the state. Large cities in the Third Reich forced Jews to work in labor gangs building roads and cleaning streets. Landlords were allowed to evict Jews on almost any pretext. After *Kristallnacht* thousands of Jews rushed to get out of Germany and Austria. Securing travel and the necessary paperwork required great perseverance and often a bit of luck.

> "I have received a letter written on the Fuhrer's orders requesting that the Jewish question be now, once and for all, coordinated and solved one way or another."[19]
>
> —Hermann Goering, a member of Hitler's inner circle.

Some with relatives in the United States, Canada, Britain, or Palestine were able to get entry visas. Others settled for more far-flung destinations, including Cuba, China, or Turkey. Many Jews who left ended up in neighboring European countries that would soon fall into Nazi hands.

Hitler and the Nazis noted certain pockets of disapproval about the events of *Kristallnacht*, even among their supporters. Some Germans expressed shame that such things could occur in a supposedly civilized nation. They had nothing but contempt for the young hooligans who delighted in others' misery. Erich Klapproth, a Protestant minister, signed a letter to Hitler and Goering in which he wrote, "But not only will I on no account justify the numerous excesses against Jewry that took place on or after Nov. 9 of this year (it is unnecessary to go into details) but I reject them, deeply ashamed, as they are a blot on the good name of the Germans."[20] Others deplored the widespread disorder and the mess left behind. News of the riots made the front pages of newspapers around the world. US president Franklin D. Roosevelt condemned the violence, and other world leaders also expressed outrage. Yet there were no economic sanctions against Nazi Germany, no cutoff of diplomatic relations, no easing of quotas for Jewish immigrants. Hitler became a bit more careful in hiding anti-Semitic violence from the eyes of the German public and the rest of the world. Yet he also realized no one was likely to come to the aid of the Jews.

Hitler's *Reichstag* Speech of 1939

In the wake of *Kristallnacht*, sections of the Nazi regime became more apocalyptic in their plans for dealing with the Jews. In an address to his SS corps, Himmler boasted of his success at exporting anti-Semitism to Nazi-controlled territory. Soon, he assured his listeners, the world would have no room for the Jews. A Nazi journal published an article titled "Jews, What Now?" in which the author stressed the lack of world reaction to the riots and claimed the screams of Jews were like a high-pitched sound that the world could no longer hear. Jews were little more than criminals and mischief-making Bolsheviks, the writer said, and should be confined to special neighborhoods away from ordinary Germans. Should the Jews rise up, they should be destroyed with fire and sword.

Hitler himself indulged in his most bloodthirsty rhetoric yet. In a speech to the German *Reichstag* on January 30, 1939, he raged for two hours about the Jewish question. *The Eternal Jew*, a Nazi propaganda film, captures the climactic moment when Hitler abandons all pretense to statesmanship and roars a terrifying prediction. "Today I will be once more a prophet: if the international Jewish financiers in and outside Europe should succeed in plunging the nations once more into a world war, then the result will not be the Bolshevizing of the earth [Communist triumph], and thus the victory of Jewry, but the annihilation of the Jewish race in Europe!"[21] The film records the hysterical applause of the

Refugees in Limbo

After *Kristallnacht* many Jews stepped up their efforts to leave Germany. For most of the 938 passengers of the transatlantic liner *St. Louis* this was the last chance to escape from the Nazis. The ship sailed from Hamburg on May 13, 1939, bound for Cuba. Most of the Jewish passengers on board had applied for visas to the United States and planned to stay in Havana until their paperwork was approved. None knew that political objections in Cuba had already made landing there unlikely. A week before the *St. Louis* sailed, Cuba's president, Federico Laredo Bru, had declared the most recently issued landing certificates to be invalid. Entry now required written permission from Cuban officials and payment of a $500 bond. At a rally in Havana attended by forty thousand supporters, a government spokesman urged the crowd to "fight the Jews until the last one is driven out."

On May 27 when the ship landed in Havana Harbor, only those passengers with valid papers were admitted. More than 900 remained in limbo, still waiting for US visas. Sympathetic stories of the Jewish refugees' plight made newspapers worldwide. Yet the United States refused to ease its restrictions on immigrants. On June 6 the *St. Louis* was forced to return to Europe. With the aid of certain Jewish organizations, entry visas were obtained from Great Britain, Belgium, the Netherlands, and France. As a result just over half the passengers of the *St. Louis* were able to survive the Final Solution.

Quoted in United States Holocaust Memorial Museum, "Voyage of the St. Louis," *Holocaust Encyclopedia*. www.ushmm.org.

Reichstag audience, typical for a speech by the Führer. No special attention was paid to Hitler's threat at the time. It was considered strictly politics, a ploy to rid the Third Reich of Jews and encourage Western nations to accept more Jewish refugees. Yet the chaos of war in Europe would soon provide Hitler the chance to back up his prophecy. What seemed an empty threat would become a murderous policy.

CHAPTER THREE

Expulsion

itler spent the early months of 1939 mouthing words of peace and planning for war. The Nazis expanded their network of concentration camps, which were already filled with young Jewish males rounded up during *Kristallnacht*, as well as others considered political enemies or antisocial outcasts. In May 1939 Hitler secured a nonaggression pact with Joseph Stalin's Soviet Union, a strategic move that seemed to contradict the Nazis' hatred for communism. The agreement prepared the way for the two rival powers to divide up eastern Europe. Meanwhile German munitions factories worked steadily to roll out tanks, trucks, bombers, and artillery pieces for the Nazi war machine.

The Invasion of Poland

Throughout the summer of 1939 the Nazis pursued a propaganda campaign against Poland, pretending the Polish government was violating the rights of ethnic Germans living there. As a final pretext, Nazi SS guards dressed in Polish military uniforms attacked a radio station on the German-Polish border. This was all the justification Hitler needed. On September 1, 1939, Nazi troops swarmed into Poland. The Nazis' technologically advanced blitzkrieg, or lightning war, overwhelmed Polish defenses. Shortly afterward Soviet forces annexed much of eastern Poland. Suddenly the Polish people—and particularly Poland's Jews—found themselves trapped between the Nazis and Soviets. Of Poland's 3 million Jews, almost two-thirds fell under Nazi control. Poland quickly became the epicenter for Nazi hatred of the Jews, a brutal trial ground for new policies of torture and death.

Hitler planned to transform Poland into a useful source of slave labor for the Nazi war effort. Ethnic Poles, considered inferior to Aryans, fit only to be servants to the master race, were to be enslaved and removed to make way for new German settlements. Hundreds of villages in western Poland were emptied by force, their inhabitants deported or shot. Germans seeking to capitalize on the invasion followed in the army's wake, taking over Polish farms and businesses. The chaos of wartime conditions enabled storm troopers and Nazi police to roam the countryside terrorizing Polish Jews. Drunken and unruly German troops rampaged through villages populated by Jews, burning their shops and houses and looting synagogues. Beatings and rapes were rampant. Orthodox Jews were shorn of their beards and forced to crawl in the streets. Large groups of Jews were rounded up, some to be immediately shot and some to be held for ransom. Those who survived fled into the woods or were sent packing to provide living space for Germans. Property belonging to Jews was stolen by non-Jewish Poles or seized by Nazi officials for their own use. The widespread violence, improvised at the outset, was soon

German soldiers watch a Polish village burn to the ground around 1940. When Germany invaded Poland in 1939, Nazi storm troopers and police roamed the countryside terrorizing the inhabitants—especially Jews— and destroying villages.

Chaim Rumkowski and Work in the Lodz Ghetto

The Jewish ghetto in the Polish city of Lodz was one of the most productive in the German *Reich*. Hans Biebow, the German administrator in charge of the Lodz ghetto, was determined to squeeze the maximum amount of labor from the ghetto inmates. Biebow set up factories and workshops to produce goods for Germany's war effort and add to the coffers of the SS. At Lodz Biebow developed a working relationship with Chaim Rumkowski, chairman of the *Judenrat*, or Council of Jewish Elders. As head of the government in the ghetto, Rumkowski decided the inhabitants were better off working for the Nazis in order to get food and supplies. In April 1940 Rumkowski convinced Biebow to let inmates produce military equipment for the Germans in exchange for food.

Rumkowski's position as leader made him a controversial figure among the inmates. He was either loved or hated—there were no lukewarm feelings. His detractors claimed he was a petty tyrant and despised him for working with the Nazis. They noted that he carried out deportation orders without protest, even those for children. When the long work hours Rumkowski had agreed to led to a strike among inmates, he punished the ringleaders by taking away their right to work and to receive rations. Yet Rumkowski's supporters insisted his efforts to make the inmates valuable to the Nazis as workers helped keep them alive—at least for a while. Rumkowski's slogan in the ghetto defined his legacy: "Labor Is Our Only Way."

Quoted in History Learning Site, "Chaim Rumkowski." www.historylearningsite.co.uk.

to become systematic and even more merciless. While previously the Nazis had pressured German and Austrian Jews to immigrate to foreign nations, now they expelled them by force to the periphery of newly captured territory. The ordeal for Jews continued to worsen.

The Polish Ghettos

Three weeks into the invasion of Poland Nazi officials took another large step that would lead to the Final Solution. Reinhard Heydrich, the head of the security police and a man whom Hitler described approvingly as iron-hearted, laid out a new policy toward Polish Jews. In a secret memo Heydrich instructed the SS *Einsatzgruppen*, or special action squads, to gather Jews and move them to large cities, where they would be restricted to residential areas called ghettos. Jews were to be isolated from the general population and degraded to the point where few would have sympathy for them. To monitor the process the *Einsatzgruppen* were to conduct a census, make an inventory of local industries and resources, and issue reports on the new arrangements. Heydrich also ordered local leaders to create Councils of Jewish Elders to enforce Nazi decrees regarding Jews and the ghettos. In the memo Heydrich several times refers to "the final aim"[22] that his orders are intended to help achieve.

Ghettos were to be located near railroads to facilitate the transporting of captured Jews. Hundreds of ghettos were created in Nazi-occupied territory, including Lodz, Lublin, and Radom in Poland, Theresienstadt in Czechoslovakia, and Vilna in Lithuania. The Polish capital of Warsaw contained what would become the largest ghetto, comprising half a million Jews. In late 1939 the Nazis considered ghettos to be holding areas where Jews would remain until Hitler and his inner circle could decide on their ultimate fate. Some Nazi officials favored deporting Jews to Madagascar, an island off the southeast coast of Africa, while others stressed the Jews' value as slave labor for the *Reich*. After a visit to one ghetto, however, Joseph Goebbels expressed the general attitude among the Nazi elite: "It is indescribable. These aren't human beings anymore, they are animals. This is no longer a humanitarian job, but a surgical one. We must make incisions here, and very radical ones at that, otherwise all of Europe will collapse from this Jewish disease."[23]

> "It is indescribable. These aren't human beings anymore, they are animals. . . . We must make incisions here, and very radical ones at that, otherwise all of Europe will collapse from this Jewish disease."[23]
>
> —Joseph Goebbels, Nazi Minister of Propaganda.

Conditions in the Ghettos

Such a perspective as Goebbels's ensured that the ghettos were basically filthy prisons and that Jews were treated little better than animals in pens. The inhabitants brought with them whatever possessions they could fit on a wagon or lug onto a train. Overcrowding in tenement buildings, where as many as ten or twelve people might occupy a single apartment, led to unsanitary conditions. Lice and rats were everywhere, and contagious diseases including typhus, cholera, and tuberculosis posed a constant danger. Food was so scarce that often only the efforts of smugglers—who risked brutal beatings—staved off starvation. The elderly could barely survive on scraps left over from rations for younger workers. Dwellings were frigid, few had running water, and those with electricity were subject to police bans on using the lights.

> "Our entire family has died, partly from lack of food and partly from spotted fever. I also had spotted fever, but I recovered. I live only to suffer a little longer and to struggle for life. How long I will be able to continue the fight I do not know."[24]
>
> —A young Jewish resident of the Lublin ghetto in Poland, writing to his brother in England.

Families did what they could to keep their spirits up, holding religious ceremonies, arranging lessons for the young, playing music, or reading poetry together. Sick with cold and hunger, children were bewildered by all the death and anguish. One Jewish boy in the Lublin ghetto wrote to his brother in England, "Our entire family has died, partly from lack of food and partly from spotted fever. I also had spotted fever, but I recovered. I live only to suffer a little longer and to struggle for life. How long I will be able to continue the fight I do not know. Please send me food parcels and any old clothes—even rags."[24] Ghettos located near trolley lines were fenced off, not only to prevent escapes but also to allow German visitors to ride by and heckle the occupants. Beggars were a common sight on the sidewalks as were dead bodies left out for the burial societies. Nazi supervisors deliberately allowed the effects of hard labor, overcrowding, malnutrition, and filthy living conditions to take their toll in Jewish deaths.

The Councils of Jewish Elders were formed to administer daily life in the ghettos. Each council consisted of twenty-four prominent Jewish leaders in the community. Their task was to see that

German commands were carried out while also acting as a sort of government: rationing meager amounts of food, arranging for necessities such as clothing and medical care when possible, and keeping some kind of order amid the chaos. The council members tried to make ghetto workshops as productive as possible, hoping labor that was valuable to the German war effort would convince the Nazis to keep the workers alive. Council members sometimes developed contacts among the Germans, enabling them to mediate on behalf of their people. In dealing with the innumerable details of

Terror shows on the faces of Jewish children who are about to be arrested for smuggling food into the Warsaw ghetto. Thousands of Jews were forced to live in crowded, filthy ghettos where food was scarce and few had running water or electricity.

daily operations in the ghetto, council chairmen could be harsh in their decisions or high-handed. Some Jews blamed council members for collaborating with the Nazis or acting as agents for their murderous plans. In reality, however, the elders had little room to maneuver. They had to follow their overseers' instructions or else face punishment themselves.

Other Victims of the Nazi Genocide

Millions of non-Jewish victims also were caught up in the Final Solution. Hitler's quest for racial and ideological purity led him to target many different groups. The T-4 program in Berlin focused on the disabled, and Nazi death squads in the Soviet Union ruthlessly murdered not only Jews but Polish gentiles and Communists. The criminal mindset that could justify genocide of Europe's Jews proved just as deadly to other disfavored classes of people. Before the invasion of Poland Hitler had ordered his commanders to kill "without pity or mercy, all men, women, and children of Polish descent or language. Only in this way can we obtain the living space we need."

One group that suffered enormous losses was the Roma, traditionally called Gypsies. Nazi ideology considered this nomadic race, which had long been persecuted, as inferior and thus unworthy to live. SS leader Heinrich Himmler started the Racial Hygiene and Population Research Center to create genealogies of the Roma and make it easier to identify them for expulsion and death. As many as half a million Roma were murdered in the Holocaust.

Large numbers of Jehovah's Witnesses were imprisoned and lost their lives at the hands of the Nazis. Hitler attacked this Christian group for its members' refusal to pledge loyalty to his regime. Purple armbands marked Jehovah's Witnesses as traitors to the Third Reich. Homosexuals were another targeted group, with ten thousand or more murdered. Overall, an estimated five million non-Jews were slaughtered by the Nazis.

Quoted in Remember.org, a People's History of the Holocaust & Genocide, "Five Million Forgotten." http://remember.org.

The T-4 Program

While Jews were being driven into ghettos, Nazi officials began new experiments with euthanasia, or so-called mercy killing. Nazi ideology had always pursued the removal of unfit or undesirable elements from the German population. The Nazis justified this goal by pointing to books such as *Allowing the Destruction of Life Unworthy of Life* (1920), written by two highly regarded German professors, and to eugenics movements in other Western nations. In 1939 Hitler authorized new programs to put this policy into effect. Doctors and midwives were ordered to report to authorities any birth of a child with disabilities. The child was then delivered to an institution for treatment. If judged by doctors unfit for life—the typical judgment in all cases—the child was killed by lethal injection and the body returned to the family. This program quickly expanded to include not only infants but older children and teenagers whose behavior was considered abnormal. Some young people were subjected to medical experiments before being murdered.

Later that same year Hitler ordered a similar program for mentally ill or physically disabled adults. Leonardo Conti, the government's top medical official, enlisted doctors, academics, nurses, social workers, and other health care personnel to implement the policy. To ensure large numbers of subjects, Conti and his staff developed a mathematical formula to determine how many people should be targeted for so-called mercy killing. The formula produced as many as seventy-five thousand eligible cases. Mental institutions received short forms with questions about a patient's number of visitors or non-Aryan blood. Decisions about euthanasia ultimately had little to do with the patient's actual condition. One doctor describes the screening process:

> Most institutions did not have enough physicians and what physicians there were, were either too busy or did not care. They delegated the selection to the nurses and the attendants. Whoever looked sick, or was otherwise a problem, was put on a list and transported to the killing center. . . . The worst thing about this business was that it produced a certain brutalization of the nursing personnel. They got to simply picking out those whom

they did not like, and the doctors had so many patients that they did not know them, and simply put their names on the list.[25]

The program was code-named T-4, referring to Tiergartenstrasse 4, the address of the Berlin villa used as its headquarters. Falsified death certificates were given to the families of the victims to help maintain the program's secrecy. Killings were at first accomplished with poisons and injections, but soon doctors sought more efficient methods. Early in 1940 the first gassings of patients were conducted at specially designated hospitals. Rumors about these killings soon reached residents nearby, who referred to the black vans used to transport victims as "ravens." Doctors who refused to follow the directives were not punished, as the regime had no problem finding willing replacements. Moral qualms subsided as the Nazis replaced doctors' Hippocratic Oath to do no harm with an oath to the glory of the Nazi state called *Gesundheit* (Health). With the successful gassing of patients, Hitler and the Nazis had found a new template for mass murder.

> "Whoever looked sick, or was otherwise a problem, was put on a list and transported to the killing center."[25]
>
> —A German doctor.

Attack on the Soviet Union and Russian Jews

By the end of 1940 the Nazis' anti-Semitic laws had spread throughout the conquered territories of western Europe, including France, Belgium, Denmark, and Holland. Captured Jews poured into Polish ghettos, which were secured by walls built with Jewish prisoners' labor. Now Hitler, his nonaggression pact with Stalin long forgotten, turned to the Soviet Union. On June 22, 1941, Nazi troops invaded Soviet territory with the intent to crush communism, subjugate the Slavs, and wipe out the Soviet Union's 3 million Jews—labeled as the "racial basis" of the Communist state. The frenzied fighting was some of the bloodiest in history. Jews who had suffered under Soviet rule in occupied lands—villagers faced with property seizures and threats of deportation to Siberian labor camps—hoped the advancing Germans would mark an improvement. Instead German troops introduced a new level of anti-Semitic atrocities.

Hitler's policy of no mercy for Jews, Communists, and other enemies was to be strictly followed by the German military, from officers to infantry. Having cut a swathe of slaughter through conquered countries with victims that included Jews, Gypsies, religious minorities, people with disabilities, and many others deemed unfit, most German troops were hardened to cruel and ruthless tactics. This attitude helped turn the Polish frontier and the Russian steppe into killing grounds. As German armies pushed into Soviet territory, the mobile killing units of the SS *Einsatzgruppen* followed behind, murdering Jews by the thousands. Initial confusion about whether women and children should be spared was cleared up by orders from the high command to show no mercy. In their zeal to smash what Hitler saw as the Jewish-Bolshevik conspiracy, the Nazis decided that the ordinary rules of war about humane treatment of prisoners and civilians did not apply. Historian Doris L. Bergen points out there was no shortage of those willing to kill:

> Many of [the German troops'] motivations for killing in the first place were undramatic. Their comrades were doing it, and they did not want to stand out; they considered it part of their job; they had gotten used to it. . . . What we do know is that Germans were not forced to be killers. Those who refused to participate were given other assignments or transferred. To this day no one has ever found a single example of a German who was executed for refusing to take part in the killing of Jews or other civilians.[26]

Deportation of German Jews

As the invasion of Russia continued, Nazi leaders prepared to deal with Jews in Germany and other parts of the *Reich*. On September 1, 1941, a new law required German Jews to wear yellow stars as badges at all times. The Nazis had required similar badges in Poland in 1939,

A law passed in 1941 required all German Jews to wear a clearly visible badge representing the symbol of Judaism, the Star of David. In the center of the star, which was printed on coarse yellow cloth with black outlines, was the word Jude (Jew) in mock-Hebraic letters.

and they were a common feature of ghettos throughout the *Reich*. The badges, printed on coarse yellow cloth with black outlines, were supposed to represent the Star of David. In the center of the crude star, printed in mock-Hebraic letters, was the German word *Jude* for Jew. Pinned to lapels or worn on armbands, the badges were meant to be a humiliating sign of inferiority and otherness. They also helped Nazi authorities identify Jews for segregation and deportation. Even children and infants had to wear the yellow stars.

Despite living under the Nuremberg Laws and other anti-Semitic measures, Jews in western Europe were to this point relatively secure—certainly in comparison to the horrors being visited on Jews in the Soviet Union. However, that was about to end. In the middle of 1941 calls arose among leading Nazis, including propaganda minister Joseph Goebbels, to remove German Jews to the east. After a British bombing raid on Hamburg, district leader Karl Kaufman wrote to Hitler requesting permission to deport the city's Jews to free up housing for Aryans whose homes were damaged. By autumn a flood of similar appeals finally convinced Hitler to authorize the forcible deportation of German Jews. As historian David Cesarani explains, "The autumn of 1941 is one of the strangest

> "To this day no one has ever found a single example of a German who was executed for refusing to take part in the killing of Jews or other civilians."[26]
>
> —Historian Doris L. Bergen.

and most difficult periods to get a hold of. . . . In the Soviet Union you have got the most radical conceivable kind of ethnic cleansing, which is the mass shooting of populations [by the Nazis], particularly the Jewish population. . . . Tens of thousands of Jews are being massacred, but people are thinking of sending Jews alive to somewhere else where they may die, but they may not."[27] At this point Hitler and other Nazi officials could assume that targeted killing was largely unnecessary, that many if not most German Jews sent eastward would eventually perish in overcrowded ghettos and work camps. Mass deportation faced certain difficulties, as German society still thought Jewish spouses of Aryans and so-called half Jews deserved some sort of protection. Yet Hitler's willingness to take this step—to uproot German Jewish families and transport them to the east—shows that he and his inner circle were close to a decision on the Final Solution.

CHAPTER FOUR

Annihilation

Nazi expectations of a rapid victory over the Soviet Union proved faulty. By the first months of 1942, with the initial invasion a tactical failure and the United States having joined the conflict, the Nazi military now faced a two-front war it was unlikely to win. Nevertheless, the Nazi effort to eliminate the Jews continued, in fact intensified. It is not known exactly when, but sometime during 1941 Hitler had authorized a scheme for the annihilation of Europe's Jews. Plans for transporting Jews eastward by rail and expanding holding facilities into death camps were already going forward throughout 1941. While the world focused on news from the battlefield, Hitler's genocide went almost unnoticed.

The Mobile Killing Units

As Hitler contemplated new, more efficient plans for murdering Jews, mobile killing units pursued their own course of slaughter in Poland, Ukraine, Latvia, Lithuania, and Estonia. The *Einsatzgruppen*, following behind the German *Wehrmacht* (armed forces) as they advanced into the Soviet Union, worked alongside battalions of Order Police to carry out mass executions of Jews. Many historians view the *Einsatzgruppen*'s activities as the first step of the Final Solution. These mobile killing squads, numbering about three thousand men in all, received plenty of logistical support from Nazi commanders, showing their status as a valued part of the German military. Support included supplies and rations, vehicles, housing, and any extra personnel needed to move prisoners. Units also received help in rounding up victims from village police and local informants.

Typically the *Einsatzgruppen* would approach a captured city or town and order Jews to be identified and assembled at collection points. From there Jews were marched or trucked to an execution site on the outskirts of the town. One Jewish girl who managed to survive a massacre in the Ukrainian town of Volochisk recalls, "As we were passing some of those streets, there were some Ukrainians who were cheering as we were walking by, and they were applauding and cheering that this, this was being done to us. We kept on walking silently without saying anything until we were out of the city."[28] Usually trenches had been dug in advance, but sometimes the victims were forced to do the digging themselves. Captives then were robbed of their valuables and told to undress. Lined up alongside the trenches, Jews were murdered with a pistol shot to the nape of the neck. The shootings might proceed for hours at a time, as the ditches filled with piled-up bodies. Hearing the pistol cracks and victims' cries echoing in the distance, villagers knew what was happening but did nothing. Sometimes collaborators volunteered to help with the slaughter. Members of the killing squads occasionally sent home photos of the corpse-filled trenches to girlfriends or family members. The number of victims was staggering. At Babi Yar, a large ravine northwest of the Ukrainian city of Kiev, more than thirty-three thousand Jews were murdered in two days in September 1941. Altogether at least one hundred thousand Jews, Communists, and captured Soviet soldiers were massacred at Babi Yar alone. An estimated 1.3 million Soviet Jews died at the hands of the *Einsatzgruppen*.

By late summer of 1941 Heinrich Himmler feared that the killing units were wearing down from the psychological strain of the mass shootings. He asked that a new means of execution be found. Soon mobile gas vans appeared on the eastern front to help with the murderous work. Each gas van was a cargo truck converted to a portable gas chamber, in which carbon monoxide from the truck's exhaust was piped in to suffocate scores of victims at once. Hitler approved the accelerated pace of the killings. On a visit to the eastern front he decided that relocating Europe's Jews was impractical—an option that in any case was probably a smokescreen for his true intentions. The T-4 Program and the mobile gas vans had given Nazi leaders a more efficient example of how to exterminate human beings. "The Führer has ordered the Final Solution of the Jewish question," Himmler would tell Rudolf Höss, the head of the

> "The Führer has ordered the Final Solution of the Jewish question. We, the SS, have to carry out this order. . . . I have therefore chosen Auschwitz for this purpose."[29]
>
> —Heinrich Himmler's instructions to Auschwitz commandant Rudolf Höss.

In Ukraine in 1941 a Nazi soldier is about to execute a man as he sits on the edge of a mass grave filled with the bodies of murdered Jews and other perceived enemies of the Third Reich. Germany's mobile killing squads massacred one hundred thousand people at Babi Yar in Ukraine.

concentration camp at Auschwitz. "We, the SS, have to carry out this order. . . . I have therefore chosen Auschwitz for this purpose."[29] The next two years would see systematic murder on a scale without precedent in history.

The Wannsee Conference

Details of the genocide's final stage took shape on January 20, 1942, at a conference held in a lakeside villa at Wannsee, an upscale suburb of Berlin. The original purpose of the conference was to determine once and for all who was to be considered a Jew. Deportations of Jewish veterans of the Great War, so-called half Jews, and Jewish spouses of Aryans had raised controversy in Germany, and some brave voices had spoken out on behalf of these individuals. By the time the conference convened, however, the agenda had changed to coordinate European-wide efforts to slaughter Jews. Among the fifteen Nazi officials in attendance were Reich Security Service chief Reinhard Heydrich, who led the meeting, and Adolf Eichmann, head of the Jewish Office of the Gestapo. These second-tier officials did not devise the Final Solution themselves at Wannsee—that decision had been made by Hitler and his inner circle some time before—but instead they worked out the details of how it would proceed. As historian Michael Burleigh describes Wannsee, "It had become a formal sit-down between mass murderers and senior civil servants."[30]

With an eye to history, Eichmann made sure that the stenographer at the meeting did not record all the mentions of killing and destruction, preferring the use of milder bureaucratic language. Heydrich announced to the group that a policy of evacuating all of Europe's Jews to the east would go into effect immediately and that he and the RSHA (Reich Security Main Office) would lead the operation. Support from all relevant agencies would be necessary. Heydrich's description of the proposed measures was meant to sound businesslike. At last Heydrich bluntly declared, "Europe will be combed of Jews from east to west."[31] He estimated that the policy would encompass more than 11 million European Jews, including those from the United Kingdom and neutral countries such as Switzerland, Sweden, and Spain. He even discussed ways of gaining control over the Jews of other Axis powers allied with Germany.

> **"Europe will be combed of Jews from east to west."**[31]
> —Reich security chief Reinhard Heydrich.

The Nazi policy of killing every Jew in Europe was code-named *Die Endlösung*, or the Final Solution. In July 1941 Hermann Goering had used these words in his orders to Heydrich to draw up a plan "showing the measures for organization and action necessary to carrying out the final solution of the Jewish question"[32] in Nazi-occupied Europe. No one at the Wannsee Conference questioned this policy or raised a word of protest. Instead they applied themselves to ironing out difficulties. Representatives of the German armed forces and the Reich Railroads were not present at the meeting, but Hitler and his ministers had already authorized their cooperation. Everyone from party officials to petty bureaucrats played a role in implementing the plan. Overall, Wannsee was an example of would-be Nazi efficiency applied to a monstrous goal.

Adolf Eichmann and Mass Deportation of Jews

After the meeting at Wannsee Adolf Eichmann accepted the task of transporting Jews eastward to transit camps or designated death camps from German-occupied regions all over Europe. In preparation for his work, Eichmann visited the death camp at Auschwitz in 1942. He discussed with Höss the details of the killing techniques used there and how many weekly shipments of prisoners it could handle. Höss later said that Eichmann believed it was his idealistic mission to exterminate Jews, a measure that would "save the German people."[33]

Eichmann approached his mission with a zealot's enthusiasm and a fanatical attention to detail. He crisscrossed Europe, consulting with Nazi-occupied governments to prepare their Jewish populations for deportation—mostly by rail but also by truck and on forced marches—either to ghettos in Poland or directly to the death camps. Eichmann was obsessed with the plan's logistics and worked to ensure that rail traffic was coordinated and the death camps received a steady supply of new victims. Typically Jews in a ghetto or holding area were lulled into false optimism with promises of work camps and improved conditions. Then they were packed into railroad cars, both passenger and freight, for a journey that might last several days. Overcrowding forced the prisoners to stand the whole way. There was no food or water. Cars were freezing cold in winter and stifling in the summer heat. Sanitary facilities amounted to a single bucket, and the stench in the enclosed cars was overpowering. Many Jews died en route to

Chelmno Survivor
Michal Podchlebnik

On June 9, 1945, Michal Podchlebnik testified to a Polish magistrate about the Nazi death camp at Chelmno. In his testimony Podchlebnik, a Jew from nearby Kolo in central Poland, describes his experiences at the camp.

I heard a German voice, he was talking to those who had just arrived, he said, "You will go to the East. There are large areas where you can work. All you have to do is to put on the clean clothes you will be given and take a shower." Some time later we heard a shuffle of bare feet in the basement near our cell. We heard the Germans shouting, "Faster, faster."

I realized they were leading the Jews to the inner grounds. Suddenly, I heard a truck door slam followed by an outburst of screaming and banging on the truck's walls. Then I heard the engine start and after six-seven minutes, when the screams fainted and died, the truck left the palace grounds. Next we were ordered to go to a large room upstairs. On the floor we could see men's clothes and women's coats and shoes scattered about. We were told to carry all the clothes and shoes to some other room quickly.

When our inmates returned from the woods in the evening, they said that they had been burying Jews from Klodawa in a common grave in the woods. They removed the corpses from large black vans, in which according to their accounts, Jews had been poisoned with exhaust fumes.

Quoted in Holocaust Education & Archive Research Team, "Michal Podchlebnik, Chelmno Survivor Testimony." www.holocaustresearchproject.org.

the camps, but dead bodies were not removed until the journey's end. German officials at the camps meticulously counted the arriving passengers, dead and alive, to make sure none had escaped. Transporting Jews in this manner diverted resources from the German war effort, but for Hitler and his henchmen this was a necessary step that could not be questioned.

The Extermination Camps

Under the plan for the Final Solution, six killing centers or death camps were built in German-occupied Poland. These included the death camps of Treblinka, Chelmno, Sobibor, and Belzec, and the combined work camps/killing centers of Majdanek and Auschwitz-Birkenau. The first mass killings by poison gas actually occurred at Chelmno on December 8, 1941, before the Wannsee Conference. Chelmno was a tiny village located on a railway line near Lodz in west central Poland. A vacant castle in the village served as the base for killing operations, with storage rooms for confiscated valuables. Jews arrived by train, then were trucked to the castle's courtyard. There a white-coated SS official told them they were bound for Germany, but first they were ushered into the castle and told to strip down and shower. A basement corridor marked as an entrance to a washroom led the captive Jews to the paneled compartment of a gas van, like those employed by the *Einsatzgruppen* in Russia. As the sealed van drove into the nearby woods, piped-in diesel exhaust asphyxiated the trapped victims. When the doors were opened, any left alive were shot and the bodies were buried in mass graves by Jewish prisoners chosen for this detail. In the spring and summer heat, when the smell of rotting bodies grew unbearable, Nazi officials brought in ovens and the corpses were exhumed and burned. Rumors of the killings at Chelmno soon reached the Lodz ghetto 30 miles (48 km) away, but inmates there were helpless to react. In its single year of operations, Chelmno saw the Nazis murder almost 150,000 Jews.

Other death camps, such as Belzec in southeastern Poland and Sobibor on the present-day eastern border, also used carbon monoxide exhaust in makeshift gas chambers. Prisoners at these camps often were led directly from cattle cars to be "disinfected" in supposed shower rooms. Frequently a few survivors of the murderous fumes

Legend:
- **E** Extermination camp
- **C** Concentration camp*
- **G** City with a ghetto
- **M** Major massacre
- Axis country or country annexed by the Axis
- Occupied by Axis
- Allied country
- Neutral country

*Includes labor, prison, and transit camps

Norway

Soviet Union (Russia)

(Estonia)

(Latvia)

North Sea

Sweden

Baltic Sea

(Lithuania)

Reichskommissariat Ostland

Denmark

Belarus

Bergen-Belsen

Netherlands

United Kingdom

West Prussia & Wartheland (Poland)

General-government (Poland)

Reichskommissariat Ukraine (Ukraine)

English Channel

Belgium

Berlin

Buchenwald

Auschwitz

Germany

Paris

France

Bohemia & Morovia (Czech Rep.)

Slovakia

Dachau

Vienna

Ostmark (Austria)

Hungary

Switzerland

Slovenia

Romania

Black Sea

Vichy France

NDH (Croatia)

Serbia

Bulgaria

Spain

Mediterranean Sea

Corsica

Italy

Rome

Adriatic Sea

Montenegro

Macedonia

Albania

Occupied Greece

Turkey

Note: dotted lines show present-day borders

remained to be dispatched by Nazi guards. Soon, however, Nazi scientists found a more reliable means of killing. They tested pellets of Zyklon B, a commercial disinfectant and insecticide that vaporized when exposed to air. The clouds of poison gas gave off a strong odor of bitter almond. When inhaled, the vapors mixed with a person's red blood cells and deprived the body of oxygen, swiftly leading to unconsciousness and death. The brand of pellets used by the Nazis contained a substance that left blue stains on the walls, stains that are still visible today in the gas chambers left standing.

Josef Mengele's Death Camp Medical Experiments

In 1942 Heinrich Himmler held a meeting to authorize secret medical experiments on inmates at the Auschwitz concentration camp. Experiments on women would involve testing methods of sterilization, including huge doses of radiation and uterine injections. Men were to be castrated with X-rays. The conference began a program of medical experiments at Auschwitz and other camps that demonstrated the casual cruelty of the Final Solution.

A central figure in these experiments was SS physician Josef Mengele. Wounded at the Russian front in 1942, Mengele used his medical training to obtain assignment to Auschwitz. He would often greet trainloads of Jewish prisoners at the transit ramps, briskly assigning them either to hard labor or immediate death. Immaculate in his white coat and polished shoes, Mengele became known among inmates as "the angel of death." He was always on the lookout for twin children, which he claimed interest in as a geneticist. His experiments on these young victims were like a sick parody of science. Mengele tried to change the children's eye color by injecting chemicals into their eyes. He bled them nearly to death or injected them with germs. He stitched together one pair of Gypsy children to create Siamese twins. Following these experiments, he would kill the children and perform autopsies on their remains. Surviving twins have testified how Mengele would earn their trust with gifts of chocolate before having them delivered to his laboratory. Mengele escaped capture after the war and lived until 1979 in Paraguay and Brazil.

Auschwitz: A Killing Factory

The most notorious of the death camps was Auschwitz. Erected in 1940 as a labor camp and detention facility for political prisoners, Auschwitz was located near the southern Polish town of Oswiecim, not far from Kraków. When Hitler and the Nazis instituted the Final

Solution, Auschwitz was expanded into a complex of three camps, one of which, at Birkenau, was a killing center. The entire facility often was referred to as Auschwitz-Birkenau. For the Nazis Auschwitz was ideal in many ways, situated near the center of German-occupied territories in Europe and close to several railways used to transport prisoners, yet still a safe distance from the front. With the camp's carefully planned system, which owed much to the efforts of Höss, Auschwitz quickly became a streamlined killing factory.

Upon arriving by train at the Auschwitz unloading ramp, captive Jews were divided into columns of men and women. White-coated SS doctors decided who was fit for labor and who was to be killed at once. The doctors made their life-or-death judgments on sight, sometimes asking a few brief questions about age and occupation. One of the key criteria in the selection process was age. As Höss later told the judges at Nuremberg, site of the postwar trials for war crimes, "Children of tender years were invariably exterminated since by reason of their youth they were unable to work."[34] Those younger than sixteen and the elderly were sent directly to the gas chambers. Pregnant women were also immediately consigned to death. About 20 percent of the newly arrived prisoners were chosen as laborers. They were assigned numbers, which were tattooed on their forearms, and transferred to one of the work camps, passing through gates bearing the ironic motto *Arbeit Macht Frei*—work makes one free. The SS actually profited from renting out these slave laborers to factories in the area.

> "Children of tender years were invariably exterminated since by reason of their youth they were unable to work."[34]
>
> —Auschwitz commandant Rudolf Höss, speaking at the Nuremberg war crimes trials.

Prisoners selected to die made their way to the gas chambers, accompanied by an escort of SS men. Those too ill or feeble to march rode in trucks. To keep prisoners quiet, SS guards calmly assured them they were only going to bathe and undergo disinfection before entering the main camp. Victims disrobed and were handed bars of soap before being locked into an airtight gas chamber disguised as a shower room. Then Zyklon B pellets were dropped inside from ceiling vents, producing rising clouds of cyanide gas. Guards knew all the victims were dead when their shouts and screams went silent.

It was left to the *Sonderkommandos*—special units of Jewish prisoners—to dispose of the dead. They dragged the corpses from the gas chambers, cut off the women's hair, and removed any rings and jewelry. Gold fillings were pried from the teeth of corpses. The bodies were burned in large pits, or later in specially built furnaces. The whole process, from the train's arrival to the disposal of bodies, took about two hours. Bones left unburned were ground with pestles, and the powder and ashes were dumped in ponds close by or scattered in surrounding fields. It is estimated that more than 1 million Jews were murdered at Auschwitz alone.

Jewish women and children arrive by train at the Auschwitz-Birkenau death camp in Poland in the early 1940s. Most were sent directly to their deaths in the gas chambers. Others died from overwork, cold, and starvation.

People in the area saw the thick columns of smoke and breathed the daily stench, watched the trains arrive full and leave empty. "Later on it was claimed that nobody knew, that nobody was guilty of anything," says Auschwitz survivor Ernst Levin. "This was impossible. The scope of the annihilation was such that it involved hundreds of thousands of people."[35] Nazi officials pursued secrecy at Auschwitz, as they did at the other death camps, but the operation was too vast to conceal. And perhaps concealment was unnecessary. There was a steady stream of civilians from Berlin and elsewhere willing to work at the facilities as needed. Nazis craved assignment to one of the camps, where every luxury was available to them and their families, not to mention an endless supply of slave labor. Working at an extermination camp was surely preferable to serving with the besieged German armies on the Russian front.

> "Later on it was claimed that nobody knew, that nobody was guilty of anything. This was impossible. The scope of the annihilation was such that it involved hundreds of thousands of people."[35]
>
> —Auschwitz survivor Ernst Levin.

CHAPTER FIVE

Liberation of the Camps and Aftermath

Despite the Nazis' efforts to conceal the truth about the Final Solution and the death camps, rumors and eyewitness accounts soon began to appear. Western nations already knew about Hitler and the Nazis' brutal anti-Semitism and prior episodes such as passage of the Nuremberg Laws and *Kristallnacht*. But the stories coming to light by 1942 were especially troubling. In late June the *New York Times* reported that Nazi death squads had shot more than 1 million Jews in occupied Russia. Also that summer a representative of the World Jewish Congress in Switzerland passed along a report from an unnamed German businessman about the mass murder of Jews. There were isolated tales of atrocities against Jews from other sources as well. "In the nature of the situation," writes historian Peter Novick, "there were no firsthand reports from Western journalists. Rather, they came from a handful of Jews who had escaped, from underground sources, from anonymous German informants, and, perhaps most unreliable of all, from the Soviet government."[36] Since the reports were scattered and contradictory, many people assumed they were exaggerated, and in the chaos of world war the progress of the fighting drew the most attention anyway. Yet urgent voices began to be heard. In December 1942 British foreign secretary Anthony Eden declared in a speech to the House of Commons that the Nazis were "now carrying into effect Hitler's oft-repeated intention to exterminate the Jewish People of Europe."[37] In March 1943 American Jews rallied in New York City's Madison Square Garden to urge the US government to take action on behalf of Europe's Jews. In general, however, people in the United States and other Allied countries were unaware of the scope of Hitler's murderous project.

The Warsaw Ghetto Uprising

Reports of what actually went on in the death camps began to leak back to the ghettos, which led some Jews to form resistance groups. In the summer of 1942, more than three hundred thousand Jews in the Warsaw ghetto—an average of six thousand a day—were transported to the Treblinka camp, 50 miles (80 km) to the northeast. The remaining inmates in Warsaw, many of them young and relatively healthy, realized that deportation meant certain death. They decided to resist at all costs. The inmates, including teenagers and women, formed a group called the ZOB—initials of the Polish words that mean Jewish Fighting Organization. When deportations began again in January 1943, Mordechai Anielewicz, the ZOB's leader, urged his fellow Jews to resist being herded to the railroad cars. Armed with weapons smuggled in from anti-Nazi Poles, ZOB squads attacked SS guards from rooftops, attic windows, and cellars. They successfully resisted deportation and forced the SS to retreat. The uprising infuriated Heinrich Himmler. Combined with harsh winter conditions and an insufficient number of trains, the attacks had forced the SS to miss its February 1943 deadlines for deporting Warsaw Jews. In retaliation for the twenty SS men killed in the fighting, Himmler ordered the massacre of one thousand Jews in the public square.

In April Himmler decided to clear the Warsaw ghetto completely in three days. The Warsaw Jews, barricaded inside tunnels and makeshift bunkers in the ghetto buildings, prepared to resist once more. On the Jewish feast day of Passover, twelve hundred ZOB fighters managed to repel the German assault in a furious battle. Finally SS general Jürgen Stroop set about burning the entire ghetto to the ground, building by building. Stroop describes the fierce resistance in a report:

> The Jews stayed in the burning buildings until because of the fear of being burned alive they jumped down from the upper stories. . . . With their bones broken, they still tried to crawl across the street into buildings which had not yet been set on fire. . . . Despite the danger of being burned alive the Jews and bandits often preferred to return into the flames rather than risk being caught by us.[38]

As the ghetto collapsed around them, the fighters somehow held out for four weeks. At the end the SS captured fifty-six thousand Jews, sending them to the Treblinka or Majdanek death camps or to forced-labor camps. A few of the fighters escaped to the forests outside Warsaw and joined Polish groups opposed to the Nazis. In the end the uprising had affirmed the spirit of the captive Jews. As Anielewicz wrote in his last letter home, "What happened is beyond our wildest dreams. Twice the Germans fled from our ghetto. . . . Only a few chosen ones will hold out; all the rest will perish sooner or later. The die is cast. . . . The main thing is: My life's dream has come true; I have lived to see Jewish resistance in the ghetto in all its greatness and glory."[39]

Efforts to Cover Up the Final Solution

Throughout 1943 and 1944 the Nazis pursued the extermination of Jews with a fanatical tenacity. The railway transports and death camp operations proceeded according to plan, regardless of German setbacks on the battlefield. The murders continued even when it meant killing skilled Jewish workers in areas where there were labor shortages. On May 19, 1943, Nazi leaders boasted that Jews had been completely eliminated from Berlin. In November Julius Streicher's *Der Stürmer* newspaper declared, "It is actually true that the Jews have, so to speak, disappeared from Europe."[40] Officially, however, the Final Solution did not exist. Orders related to the killing generally were verbal. Little was written down, and what few documents addressed the killing process were classified as top secret. Hitler and his henchmen relied on code names and euphemisms. "Special treatment" and "action," for example, indicated violence directed against Jews or some other group. Aktion Reinhard, named after Reinhard Heydrich, served as code name for the extermination of Polish Jewry in specially built death camps. The constant use of code names and indirect references suggests that upper level Nazis knew the enormity of their crimes. Hermann Goering, founder of the

"My life's dream has come true; I have lived to see Jewish resistance in the ghetto in all its greatness and glory."[39]

—Mordechai Anielewicz, leader of the Jewish resistance in the Warsaw Ghetto.

Nazi forces round up Jews in the Warsaw ghetto in May 1943. Angered by a ghetto uprising that resulted in the deaths of twenty SS members and a temporary halt in deportations, SS chief Heinrich Himmler ordered the execution of one thousand Jews in the public square.

Gestapo secret police, said as much: "We will go down in history either as the world's greatest statesmen or its worst villains."[41]

The Nazis and their collaborators also sought to destroy evidence of the Final Solution by disposing of the victims' corpses. This was the reason for the crematoria in the death camps, the reason that mass graves in Poland and Ukraine were dug up so that piles of bodies could be set aflame and burned to ashes. Such efforts took on extra urgency in 1944 when Soviet armies advanced toward the sites of the massacres. A famous example of Nazi subterfuge occurred that summer in what is now the Czech Republic. The Nazis allowed a group from the International Red Cross to visit Terezin (also called Theresienstadt), which was touted as a model ghetto. Nazi propaganda declared that Hitler had built the village solely to protect Jews from the terrors of war. To fool the visitors SS officials spruced up the site by painting houses, planting gardens, and arranging shops and cafés along

Jewish Children in Hiding

As the stages of the Final Solution became more deadly, many Jews sought to save themselves by hiding from the Nazis. Deportation orders left Jewish families facing a dilemma. They could attempt to flee, seek hiding places, or try to pass themselves off as gentiles. In Poland more than one hundred thousand Jews lived in hiding, of which perhaps half survived to the war's end. Jewish parents often chose to hide their children, meaning families faced the agonizing step of being separated. Children were easier to hide for several reasons. Non-Jewish families who agreed to harbor refugees generally felt more sympathetic to children than adults. Also, children required less food and space than adults and caused fewer disruptions to home life. Jewish parents hoped that host families could be trusted with their children's safety.

The hosts themselves faced dire consequences if caught harboring Jews, including deportation to labor camps, destruction of their homes, and sometimes death. Even neighbors could be in peril. Paulette Pomeranz was a young Jewish girl whose mother placed her in hiding with a family near Athens, Greece. As she recalls, "The townspeople were frightened too. Although I was the only Jewish person in the neighborhood, they knew that if the Germans found out, we'd all be shot. Yet they did everything to help me." Emotional trauma continued after the war as well, with Jewish children often feeling alienated from their real parents—if their parents were still alive—and host families grieving over the children's departure.

Quoted in Maxine B. Rosenberg, *Hiding to Survive: Stories of Jewish Children Rescued from the Holocaust*. New York: Clarion, 1994, p. 13.

the main boulevard. In reality, many prisoners at Terezin had been evacuated to death camps shortly before to make the ghetto seem less crowded. After the Red Cross's six-hour visit—resulting in a positive report—the SS resumed deportations from Terezin to Auschwitz with a vengeance.

Liberation of the Death Camps

Propaganda could not change the fact that the tide of the war had turned. On June 6, 1944, Allied troops landed on Normandy Beach in France. At the same time Russian forces continued to push the German army back across the former Polish border. On July 23, 1944, Soviet troops liberated the Majdanek extermination camp at Lublin in eastern Poland. Anticipating the Red Army's advance, Nazi officials had hastily removed fifteen thousand Jewish prisoners westward by train to Auschwitz, Ravensbrück, and other death camps. A final group of one thousand Jews were marched out on foot the day before the Russians arrived. The Nazis had also burned down the large crematorium used to incinerate the dead bodies of victims but left standing the gassing facility. Russian soldiers were thus the first of the Allies actually to see a gas chamber. (Reports of their existence had been broadcast on the BBC two years earlier.) The Soviets filmed the mostly deserted camp, focusing at one point on a pile of shoes—eight hundred thousand shoes—taken from Jewish prisoners.

In the summer of 1944 the Soviets liberated more camps in Poland, including Belzec, Treblinka, and Sobibor. In January 1945 they reached Auschwitz. Only a few thousand huddled prisoners were left alive at this site where more than a million Jews had been murdered. Nazi guards had given inmates the choice of staying behind in the camp or following them on foot westward through two feet of snow. This practice became known as the death march, because prisoners who faltered on the way were shot and left on the roadside. Soviet troops entering Auschwitz discovered many signs of the camp's grisly business. A few frozen corpses were found in a shed, the victims having died too late to be cremated while the ovens were still operating. Much of the camp had been dismantled and camp records burned, but a few warehouses remained. Inside, the Soviets found mountainous piles of personal belongings, including hundreds of thousands of women's dresses and men's suits. One warehouse held nearly fifteen thousand pounds of human hair.

> "We will go down in history either as the world's greatest statesmen or its worst villains."[41]
>
> —Hermann Goering, founder of the Gestapo secret police.

As British and American forces pushed into Germany they also began to liberate camps. Those liberated by British troops included Bergen-Belsen in northwest Germany, where about one hundred thousand Jews and other prisoners lost their lives from starvation, diseases such as typhus, and gunshots to the neck. Soon after the liberation at Bergen-Belsen, *LIFE* magazine published photos and eyewitness accounts of what the soldiers found: a road lined with dead bodies; hundreds of shrouded corpses lying in a stand of trees; piles of naked corpses loaded onto trucks;

When British soldiers liberated Bergen-Belsen in April 1945, among the many horrific sights that greeted them was a road lined with dead bodies. Before them, in a stand of trees, lay hundreds of shrouded corpses.

a mass grave filled to the brim with dead victims; dying women huddled on the bare ground behind barbed wire. *LIFE*'s editors referred to a "barbarism that reaches the low point of human degradation."[42] The pictures confirmed the worst of the rumors and partial accounts that had filtered out during the war. For the first time, millions of readers confronted the truth about Hitler's Final Solution.

On April 11, 1945, American troops encountered similar scenes when they liberated the Buchenwald camp near Weimar, Germany. Buchenwald lacked gas chambers, but thousands of Jewish prisoners had died there from malnutrition, disease, medical experiments, beatings, and executions. Harry Snodgrass, a young soldier from Tennessee, toured the camp in disbelief two days after its liberation. "It was in the commander's office," he said. "There were lampshades made from the skin of Jews. In the crematorium they used the ashes of the inmates to fertilize the fields—the ashes of dead people. After an hour, it just became too much. I was stunned—just stunned. We don't even treat dogs like this."[43] At the end of April US soldiers entered the notorious camp at Dachau in Bavaria. They set about transferring weak and dying prisoners to hospital facilities and distributing food to those able to eat. As historian Abram Sachar writes,

> "There were lampshades made from the skin of Jews. . . . They used the ashes of the inmates to fertilize the fields—the ashes of dead people. . . . I was stunned—just stunned. We don't even treat dogs like this."[43]
>
> —US soldier Harry Snodgrass, after liberating Buchenwald concentration camp.

One of the German guards came forward to surrender with what he believed would be the usual military protocol. He emerged in full regalia, wearing all his decorations. . . . He saluted and barked "Heil Hitler." An American officer looked down and around at mounds of rotting corpses, at thousands of prisoners shrouded in their own filth. He hesitated only a moment, then spat in the Nazi's face, snapping "Schweinehund [pig-dog]," before ordering him taken away. Moments later a shot rang out and the American officer was informed that there was no further need for protocol.[44]

The Nuremberg Trials

As Allied forces closed in on Berlin and the Nazi regime collapsed, violence against Jews continued. One by one the Nazis evacuated the concentration camps and forced thousands of prisoners to make death marches back into Germany. Shootings and beatings of Jews, many from Nazi-allied Hungary, stopped only with Germany's surrender on May 7, 1945. Holed up in his Berlin bunker, Adolf Hitler wrote his final testament, railing against the Jews to the end. He killed himself rather than face retribution for his crimes.

With the war in Europe over, the Allies assembled the International Military Tribunal (IMT) in Nuremberg, Germany to try high-level Nazis. The IMT included judges from the United States, Great Britain, France, and the Soviet Union. The defendants were charged in three categories, including crimes against humanity—"namely, murder, extermination, enslavement, deportation, and other inhumane acts committed against any civilian population, before or during the war."[45] Two members of Hitler's inner circle, Heinrich Himmler and Josef Goebbels, had committed suicide months before the trial began. Among the twenty-four Nazis indicted were Hitler's second-in-command Hermann Goering, deputy führer Rudolf Höss, armaments minister Albert Speer, and publisher Julius Streicher. Most observers hailed Nuremberg as a milestone in international justice, although a few demurred, such as US Supreme Court justice Harlan Stone, who called it a "sanctimonious fraud"[46] and questioned its legitimacy according to common law. At the end all but three of the defendants were found guilty and twelve were hanged. Goering escaped hanging by taking a cyanide capsule the night before. Subsequent war crime trials dealt with minor Nazi officials, military officers, and German industrialists.

The Trial of Eichmann

The Final Solution and Nazi war crimes faded from public concern during the 1950s. Jewish refugees and survivors of the ghettos and concentration camps had crisscrossed Europe in search of places where they would be free from anti-Semitic prejudice. Some faced further violence when they tried to return to towns and villages in Poland and elsewhere in Eastern Europe. By 1953 the new Jewish state of Israel had welcomed

In January 1946 major Nazi figures including Gestapo founder Hermann Goering (front row, far left) listen to proceedings of the Nuremberg Trials. During the trials a panel of judges (and the world) heard details of Nazi atrocities and roles the defendants played in them.

an estimated 170,000 displaced Jews. Other refugees waited for visas to the United States, Canada, Mexico, South America, or Australia. In these years the search for Nazi perpetrators of the Final Solution lost priority in the West to fears about the Cold War and nuclear weapons.

It took an incident in Argentina on May 11, 1960, to bring attention once more to the Final Solution. That night operatives for Mossad, the Israeli intelligence force, kidnapped former Nazi Adolf Eichmann as he returned to his home on the outskirts of Buenos Aires. Eichmann, who had worked tirelessly for the SS to arrange the deportation and mass murder of Jews, was flown back to Israel to stand trial. The proceedings took place in a Jerusalem courtroom before a worldwide audience in 1961. Sitting in a bulletproof glass box, Eichmann listened to the emotional testimony of death camp survivors. He told the judges he was merely "a tool in the hands of stronger powers"[47] and asked Jews for mercy and understanding. Eichmann was convicted on numerous charges and sentenced to death. His hanging on June 1, 1962, is the only execution ever conducted by Israel.

Eichmann and the Banality of Evil

In 1963 German Jewish philosopher Hannah Arendt published an explosive series of articles in the *New Yorker* magazine on the trial in Israel of the war criminal Adolf Eichmann. While attending the trial, Arendt was struck by how unimpressive Eichmann was. He seemed no evil fanatic but rather an ordinary elderly man who claimed to have been merely a cog in the larger Nazi wheel. This led Arendt to coin the famous phrase "the banality of evil" to describe Eichmann, and by extension the Final Solution itself. (*Banality* means boring or unimaginative.) She seemed to be saying that the Holocaust was perpetrated mainly by desk murderers—ordinary bureaucrats just following orders. The articles, collected in the book *Eichmann in Jerusalem*, set off a firestorm of controversy. Some reviewers attacked Arendt for minimizing Eichmann's responsibility. Others agreed with her idea that the Final Solution had more to do with totalitarian systems than with Hitler and the Nazis' anti-Semitism.

In her recent book *Eichmann Before Jerusalem*, German author Bettina Stangneth disputes Arendt's claims. Stangneth focuses on tapes Eichmann made in Argentina while in hiding after the war. In the tapes, made with a group of ex-Nazis, Eichmann reveals himself to be a fanatical anti-Semite with no regrets for his actions: "If we had killed 10.3 million, I would be satisfied, and would say, good, we have destroyed an enemy." Stangneth's research promises to renew the debate about the meaning of the Final Solution.

Quoted in Gerald Steinacher, "Extraordinary Evil," *Wall Street Journal*, October 14, 2014. http://online.wsj.com.

The Final Solution Today

Adolf Hitler and the Nazis' attempt to exterminate Europe's Jews remains the most notorious event of the twentieth century. The Nazis' bureaucratic code words Final Solution continue to have a sinister cast in the public mind. Films such as *Sophie's Choice*, *Schindler's List*,

The Pianist, and the television miniseries *Holocaust* have dramatized the plight of Jews under the Nazi regime to inform later generations about the atrocities that occurred on a daily basis. Documentary films such as *Shoah* preserve the accounts of death camp survivors, and books examining all aspects of the Final Solution are found in every library. Yet still some so-called Holocaust deniers insist that the murders never occurred or were much less extensive than portrayed.

> "Those who cannot remember the past are condemned to repeat it."[48]
> —Philosopher George Santayana.

With even the youngest survivors and eyewitnesses now aging, it is important that their stories are not lost. As the philosopher George Santayana warns, "Those who cannot remember the past are condemned to repeat it."[48]

Introduction: A Speech on an Age-Old Hatred

1. Quoted in Erik Kirchbaum and Bethan John, "At a Landmark Berlin Rally, Merkel Vows to Fight Anti-Semitism," Reuters, September 14, 2014. www.reuters.com.

2. Quoted in Micki Weinberg, "Wave of Anti-Semitic Rallies Hits Cities Across Germany," *Times of Israel*, July 21, 2014. www.timesofisrael.com.

3. Quoted in Theo Bailey, "Understanding the German People's Participation in the Third Reich," *Ampersand*, Florida Gulf Coast University, April 1999. http://itech.fgcu.edu.

4. Quoted in American Council for Judaism, "Jewish Assimilation: Berlin as a Showcase," Summer 2000. www.acjna.org.

Chapter One: Hatred and Exclusion

5. Quoted in Alpha History, "Nazi Anti-Semitism." http://alphahistory.com.

6. Quoted in Jewish Virtual Library, "Adolf Hitler: Excerpts from *Mein Kampf*." www.jewishvirtuallibrary.org.

7. Quoted in History Place, "Holocaust Timeline." www.historyplace.com.

8. Quoted in Michael Burleigh, *The Third Reich: A New History*. New York: Hill and Wang, 2000, p. 285.

9. Quoted in Owlnet, "The Nuremberg Race Laws." www.owlnet.rice.edu.

10. Nathan Stoltzfus, *Resistance of the Heart: Intermarriage and the Rosenstrasse Protest in Nazi Germany*. New Jersey: Rutgers University Press, 2001, p. 68.

11. Quoted in Burleigh, *The Third Reich*, p. 295.

12. Quoted in Jewish Virtual Library, "The Nuremberg Laws: Background & Overview." www.jewishvirtuallibrary.org.

Chapter Two: Persecution

13. Quoted in Children in History, "Nazi Anschluss: Actions Against Jews (March 1938)." http://histclo.com.

14. Stefan Zweig, *The World of Yesterday*. New York: Viking, 1943, p. 405.

15. Quoted in Alpha History, "Jewish Property Seizures." http://alphahistory.com.

16. Quoted in United States Holocaust Memorial Museum, "Kristallnacht: A Nationwide Pogrom, November 9–10, 1938." www.ushmm.org.

17. Quoted in Eric A. Johnson, *What We Knew: Terror, Mass Murder, and Everyday Life in Nazi Germany*. Cambridge, MA: Basic Books, 2005, pp. 27–28.

18. Quoted in Burleigh, *The Third Reich*, p. 330.

19. Quoted in Jewish Virtual Library, "Kristallnacht: Background & Overview." www.jewishvirtuallibrary.org.

20. Quoted in Burleigh, *The Third Reich*, p. 332.

21. Quoted in Hans Mommsen, "Hitler's Reichstag Speech of 30 January 1939," *History & Memory*, Fall 1997, p. 147.

Chapter Three: Expulsion

22. Quoted in Nizkor Project, "Letter from Heydrich to the Chiefs of All Einsatzgruppen Concerning 'The Jewish Question in the Occupied Territories,' 21 September, 1939," in *The Einsatzgruppen*. www.nizkor.org.

23. Quoted in Skepticism, "Goebbels Visits Lodz Ghetto While Traveling Through Conquered Areas of Poland." http://skepticism.org.

24. Quoted in JTA, "Jewish Children in Polish Ghettos Plead for Food and Clothes." www.jta.org.

25. Quoted in Life: A New Zealand Resource for Life Related Issues, "Euthanasia in Nazi Germany—The T4 Programme." www.life.org.nz.

26. Doris L. Bergen, *The Holocaust: A Concise History*. Lanham, MD: Rowman & Littlefield, 2009, p. 158.

27. Quoted in WW2History.com, "German Jews Deported." http://ww2history.com.

Chapter Four: Annihilation

28. Quoted in United States Holocaust Memorial Museum, "Einsatzgruppen (Mobile Killing Units)—Oral History," *Holocaust Encyclopedia*. www.ushmm.org.

29. Quoted in History Place, "The Nazi Holocaust 1938–1945—6,000,000 Deaths." www.historyplace.com.

30. Burleigh, *The Third Reich*, p. 646.

31. Quoted in History Place, "Adolf Eichmann." www.historyplace.com.

32. Quoted in David White and Daniel P. Murphy, "The Final Solution," Netplaces. www.netplaces.com.

33. Quoted in PBS, "Adolf Eichmann (1906–1962)," *American Experience*. www.pbs.org.

34. Quoted in Nizkor Project, "Persecution of the Jews." www.nizkor.org.

35. Quoted in Johnson, *What We Knew*, p. 81.

Chapter Five: Liberation of the Camps and Aftermath

36. Peter Novick, "Chapter One: The Holocaust in American Life," *New York Times*. www.nytimes.com.

37. Quoted in History Place, "The Nazi Holocaust 1938–1945—6,000,000 Deaths."

38. Quoted in William L. Shirer, *Rise and Fall of the Third Reich: A History of Nazi Germany*. New York: Simon and Schuster, 1990, p. 977.

39. Quoted in Simple to Remember: Judaism Online, "The Final Solution." www.simpletoremember.com.

40. Quoted in Children in History, "Biography: Julius Streicher (1885–1946)." http://histclo.com.

41. Quoted in *Hitler's Children*, "Goering Quotes," documentary. www.hitlerschildren.com.

42. Quoted in *LIFE*, "At the Gates of Hell: The Liberation of Bergen-Belsen, April 1945." http://life.time.com.

43. Quoted in Scrapbook Pages, "Liberation of Buchenwald Concentration Camp." www.scrapbookpages.com.

44. Quoted in Nizkor Project, "The Liberation of Dachau." www.nizkor.org.

45. Quoted in United States Holocaust Memorial Museum, "The Nuremberg Trials," The Holocaust: A Learning Site for Students. www.ushmm.org.

46. Quoted in *History*, "Nuremberg Trials." www.history.com.

47. Quoted in Gerald Steinacher, "Extraordinary Evil," *Wall Street Journal*, October 15, 2014. http://online.wsj.com.

48. George Santayana, *The Santayana Edition: The Critical Edition of the Works of George Santayana*, Indiana University–Purdue University. http://lat.iupui.edu.

Hannah Arendt

A German Jewish writer and philosopher who described Adolf Eichmann's bureaucratic role in the Final Solution as "the banality of evil."

Adolf Eichmann

Head of the Office for Jewish Emigration in Vienna, Austria, and later chief of the Jewish Office of the Gestapo. Eichmann played a crucial role in organizing the forced deportation of Jews throughout Nazi-occupied territory to ghettos and death camps in Poland. Eichmann's capture and trial for war crimes in Israel drew worldwide attention in the early 1960s.

Joseph Goebbels

The minister of propaganda in the Nazi government. He concocted stories about an international conspiracy of Jewish financiers and used a variety of media to declare the supposed inferiority of Jews. He also promoted the idea that Aryan Germans were the master race. A true believer in Nazism, Goebbels committed suicide alongside Hitler in 1945.

Hermann Goering

A top Nazi official and head of the German *Luftwaffe* (air force). Goering was once Hitler's second-in-command but lost his support after Germany's military failures in 1942.

Roman Grynspan

A seventeen-year-old Polish Jew whose shooting of a German embassy official in Paris was used by Hitler as pretext for the violence of *Kristallnacht*.

Reinhard Heydrich

Chief of the Reich Security Service in the Nazi regime. Heydrich chaired the notorious Wannsee Conference in which details of the Final Solution were discussed and approved.

Heinrich Himmler

The leader of the elite Nazi guard called the *Schutzstaffel* (SS). Himmler has been labeled the architect of the Final Solution for his control over the network of agencies that implemented the Nazi policy of murdering Jews.

Adolf Hitler

Leader of the National Socialist (Nazi) Party; became chancellor of Germany in 1933. Hitler thought Jews were racially inferior yet cunning and traitorous. Hitler's vicious anti-Semitism led him to seek the annihilation of Europe's Jews with a policy referred to as the Final Solution.

Rudolf Höss

Served as commandant of the Auschwitz-Birkenau extermination camp. Höss was instrumental in organizing the systematic murder of Jews in the gas chambers of Auschwitz.

Franklin D. Roosevelt

United States president during World War II. Roosevelt condemned anti-Semitic violence in Germany and helped lead the Allies to victory over Nazi Germany.

Kurt von Schuschnigg

The leader of Austria's Fascist government when Hitler annexed Austria in the *Anschluss*. Von Schuschnigg's mild anti-Semitism subsequently gave way to the Nazis' more virulent form.

Julius Streicher

An early member of the Nazi Party and publisher of the anti-Semitic newspaper *Der Stürmer*. Streicher contributed to Hitler's Final Solution with his paper's depictions of Jews as predators, snakes, and vermin.

Books

Michael Burleigh, *The Third Reich: A New History*. New York: Hill and Wang, 2000.

David Cesarani, *Becoming Eichmann: Rethinking the Life, Crimes, and Trial of a "Desk Murderer."* Cambridge, MA: Da Capo, 2006.

Barbara Engelking and Jacek Leociak, *The Warsaw Ghetto: A Guide to the Perished City*. New Haven, CT: Yale University Press, 2009.

Eric A. Johnson and Karl-Heinz Reuband, *What We Knew: Terror, Mass Murder, and Everyday Life in Nazi Germany—an Oral History*. Cambridge, MA: Basic Books, 2005.

Ian Kershaw, *Hitler, the Germans, and the Final Solution*. New Haven, CT: Yale University Press, 2008.

Timothy W. Ryback, *Hitler's First Victims: The Quest for Justice*. New York: Alfred A. Knopf, 2014.

Internet Sources

Ofer Aderet, "For First Time, Rare Warsaw Ghetto Uprising Diaries Unveiled," *Haaretz*, January 17, 2013. www.haaretz.com.

Daniel Bates, "The Birth of the Final Solution: Hitler's Earliest Letter Which Reveals His Plans to Exterminate Jews Goes on Display for the First Time," *Mail Online*, June 7, 2011. www.dailymail.co.uk.

Gord McFee, "When Did Hitler Decide on the Final Solution?," Holocaust-History.org. www.holocaust-history.org/hitler-final-solution.

William D. Rubenstein, "The Origins of the Final Solution," *First Things*, June 2004. www.firstthings.com.

Ken Spiro, "The Final Solution," Simple to Remember: Judaism Online. www.simpletoremember.com/articles/a/the_final_solution.

Websites

History Learning Site (www.historylearningsite.co.uk). This website offers brief, focused articles on the Final Solution, such as the Polish ghettos, the Nazi transport system for Jewish prisoners, and the concentration camps.

The History Place (www.historyplace.com/worldwar2/holocaust). This website features a detailed time line of the events in the Holocaust and extensive sections on various topics related to the Final Solution.

Jewish Virtual Library (www.jewishvirtuallibrary.org). This website includes an overview of the Final Solution and reference material on the background of the events. Separate articles address topics such as the Wannsee Conference, Nazi means of mass murder, and medical experiments in the camps.

Slideshare (www.slideshare.net/echrisopoulos/steps-leading-to-the-final-solution). This website includes an extensive slide presentation of the steps leading to the Final Solution.

United States Holocaust Memorial Museum (www.ushmm.org/learn). This website features informative articles on every aspect of the Final Solution, from the rise of Hitler and Nazism to the Nuremberg Trials.

INDEX

9027